THE ZODIAC YEAR

A STARGAZER'S GUIDE TO THE ASTROLOGICAL CALENDAR

ALISON DAVIES

Illustrated by
Megan Ivy Griffiths

quadrille

MANAGING DIRECTOR
Sarah Lavelle

EDITORIAL DIRECTOR
Harriet Butt

EDITORIAL ASSISTANT
Ellie Spence

DESIGNER
Alicia House

ILLUSTRATOR
Megan Ivy Griffiths

HEAD OF PRODUCTION
Stephen Lang

PRODUCTION CONTROLLER
Martina Georgieva

Published in 2024 by Quadrille Publishing Limited

Quadrille
52–54 Southwark Street
London SE1 1UN
quadrille.com

Cataloguing in Publication Data: a catalogue record for
this book is available from the British Library.

ISBN 978 1 837 83 262 0

Printed in China using vegetable-based ink

FSC
www.fsc.org
MIX
Paper | Supporting
responsible forestry
FSC® C018179

WELCOME

On a clear night, when the world is plunged into darkness, and the gentle haze of the Moon's glow illuminates the vista, you'll be able to see the pinprick of tiny stars flickering in the distance. A spiderweb of glittering dots so startlingly bright you can pick them out with the naked eye, and yet the reality is they are millions of years and even more miles away. That fact in itself is enough to stretch the mind and the consciousness, but there are no limits to time and space, and the cosmos is a curious place where a myriad of myths and magical tales play out.

This spectral dance goes on above our heads, and often without our knowledge, for the daytime realm has a habit of taking over. Yet, to the Ancients, those night skies were more important than anything, being the gateway to the universe and a way of making sense of their surroundings. They came to rely upon the stars as a tool for navigation, and to chart the days and seasons. They realized there was a pattern to their movements, and that certain clusters and star groupings took prominence at different times of the year, some marking the coming of spring, others hailing the brooding form of winter as it crept through the landscape. Each constellation took its turn in the spotlight, returning at the same time during the turn of the wheel to provide a marker, and a way for those early civilizations to create the calendar of the year that our current calendar is based upon.

Each starry pattern, with its unique shape, told a story that elaborated on these seasonal appearances, and served the already evolving mythology of that time. It started with the Babylonians, who divided the sky into twelve areas, assigning a pattern of stars and a character to each depending on when the Sun passed through it. They were the first to chart the constellations, giving them names and even more significance. With every tale there was a moral or a lesson to be learnt, something that those first tribes could use to create order and structure, and build a civilization. The ancient Greeks then took over, borrowing from those early fragments of narrative to create their own constellation myths, and recording the stars and newly assigned zodiac signs, and when they occurred throughout the year. Their astronomers believed the skies above were governed by the gods, and that the constellations were heavenly depictions of their feats. They read much into the shifting cosmic landscape, and saw each new development as a sign, or an omen. Their tendency for superstition and magic influenced their calculations, and led to more defined outlines of the zodiac signs, along with the characteristics and governing planets that we recognize today.

The planets were gifted Roman names to correspond with the days of the week, and just like the ancient Greeks, they took their inspiration from the deities they worshipped. Each one was assigned a god, but while the constellations were based on Greek myths, the planets were charted by European astronomers who spoke and wrote primarily in Latin, the language of the Roman Empire. And so the celestial landscape became an object of fascination for the years that followed, as too were the signs of the zodiac, and their influence upon our lives.

Today, we may know our zodiac sign and have an idea of what it means, but the roots of the story and the constellation that it comes from is often shrouded in mystery. This book helps you look beyond the sparkling surface and learn the stories of the stars, taking a month-by-month journey into the related zodiac sign (also known as a sun sign), and its constellation. Starting at the very beginning with a description of what to look for in the sky, and any curious and quirky details that stand out, it then delves deeper into the Greek myth associated with the constellation of the same name, and any other folklore. While the sky showcases specific constellations each season, which are outlined in the seasonal introductions, the wheel of the zodiac calendar may not exactly match up, so while you might be gazing at Cancer in the sky, you could also be celebrating the Zodiac month of Aries.

Each section highlights the zodiac sign's governing planet and its corresponding Roman deity, and the influence this has on people born under that sign. There's a monthly zodiac ritual, which will help you harness some of the qualities and gifts attributed to the sign, and a planetary ritual to help you attune with the cosmic energy at work. For those interested in connecting with the celestial vista at a deeper level, there's a section on star bathing and star gazing at the back of this book, which looks at the basics you'll need to get started. Finally, there's a guide to the most prominent and visible constellation each month, so that you know what to look out for as you navigate the stars.

This book offers you a glimpse of the night sky and the wonders woven by the stars. It urges you to step outside and embrace the liquid darkness of the heavens; to look up, and drink in the mystical beauty of the constellations; and to understand what those who went before saw and appreciated. Through the myths and narratives of the past and the skies of the present, you can make of the most of the here and now, and enjoy this zodiac year.

SPRING

Hope reigns eternal as spring peeks a sleepy head over the horizon, bringing with it lighter, brighter days, and the gentle awakening of the earth. Movement is afoot, and not just in the changing landscape. The skies too are shifting, and the starry patterns that were starkly prominent during the winter months are moving westward. In their place come new constellations with no need to announce their arrival, even if they are tentative at first.

The constellation of Cancer the crab cautiously makes it way in the form an upside-down Y, bordering the winter constellation of Gemini to the west. Then comes Leo the lion with its sickle-shaped head. Not one to lurk in the shadows, it is one of the easiest constellations to spot at this time of year and sits neatly between Cancer to the west and Virgo to the east. Virgo also lights up the sky, being the second largest constellation in the heavens at this seasonal juncture. Her presence is all the reminder you need that the cycles of life roll onwards and warmth will soon return to the land.

While the constellation calendar shifts, so too does the zodiac calendar, beginning with the charge of Aries, a call to arms for the zodiac year, followed in its wake by the charging bull of Taurus and Gemini the astral twins.

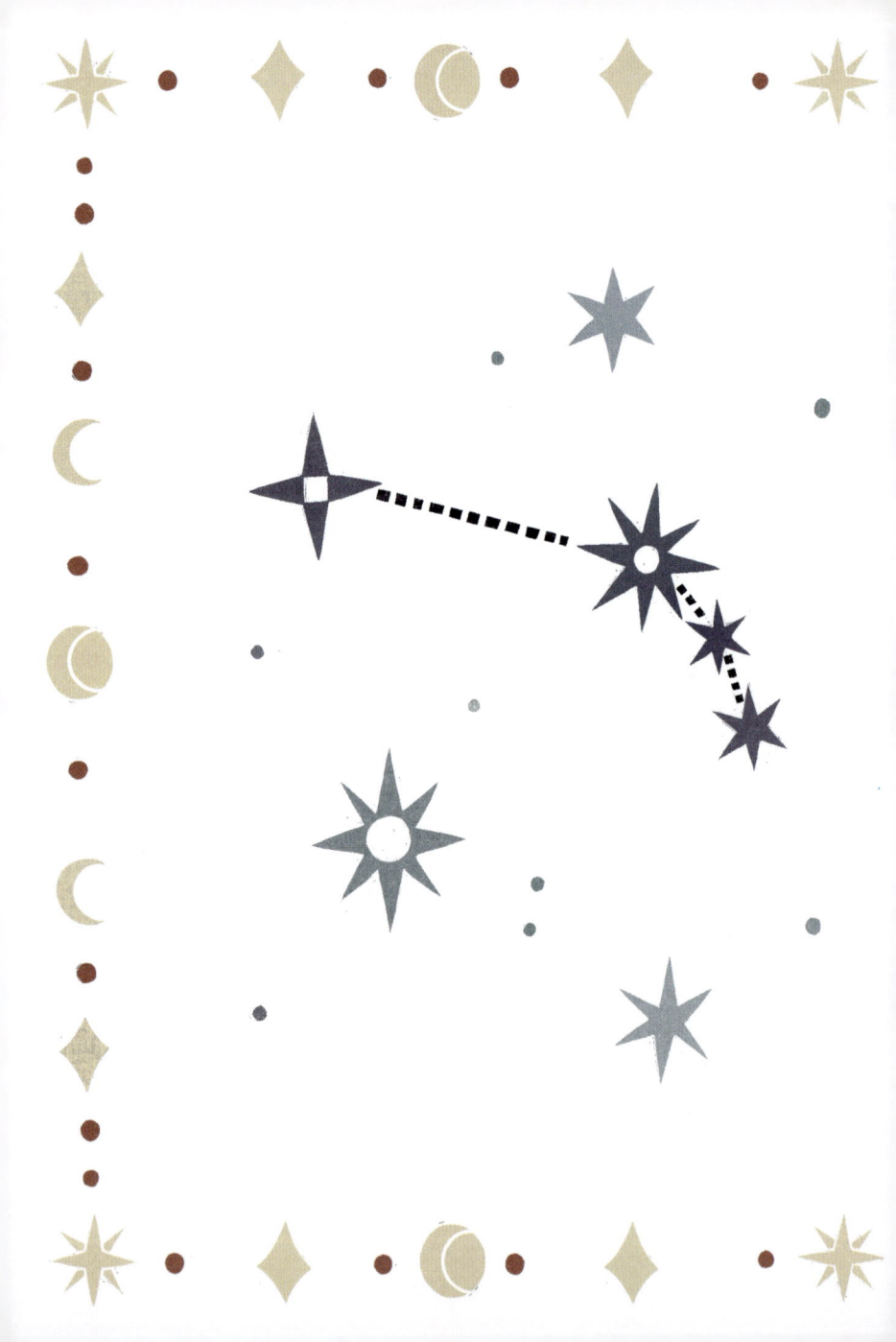

ARIES

MARCH 21ˢᵀ TO APRIL 19ᵀᴴ

ARIES THE RAM

Best Time to View: December

A faint glimmering pattern in the sky, the constellation of Aries the ram is pinned together by two bright stars – Hamal the orange giant, which is larger than the Sun, and Sheratan, the second brightest of the duo. While it is not the biggest or boldest of the constellations, when these star patterns were first named it was Aries that stood proudly at the front, illuminated by the Sun's rays during the vernal equinox. As such, this makes the sign of Aries the leader of the twelve signs of the zodiac, the first sign of the zodiac year, and a herald of spring.

THE WINGED RAM

According to Greek legend, the Boeotian king Athamas was betrothed to Nephele, a beautiful cloud nymph, and had two children with her: a boy named Phrixus and a girl named Helle. But being fickle at heart and easily led, the king strayed and pledged his heart to another younger woman, Ino. While she was happy being the new queen, she hated her stepchildren, and hatched a plan to not only destroy the land and cause the crops to fail, but also put an end to the king's children. She urged her husband to consult the Oracle for a solution to the famine that she had created by roasting the grain before it was planted. She then bribed one of his servants to lie and say that the Oracle had decreed his children should be sacrificed to save the people.

Nephele, being made of clouds and present everywhere, got wind of the plan, and asked the gods for assistance. This came in the form of a giant winged ram who swept the children from their beds and carried them to King Aeetis of Colchis. While Helle did not survive the journey, falling to her doom in the sea, Phrixus arrived safely and at the request of the honourable ram, sacrificed the creature and gave its golden hide to Aeetes. The enchanted fleece hung from a thousand-year-old oak tree in the grove of Ares, where it was guarded by a dragon.

The king of the gods Zeus was so impressed by the ram's courage and swift action that he transformed it into an array of stars, the constellation known as Aries.

FOLKLORE FROM AROUND THE WORLD

THE GOLDEN FLEECE

The Babylonians first named Aries 'the Hired Man', or 'the Agrarian Worker'. In this original form the constellation was associated with their god of shepherds, Dumuzi, and became a symbol of the spring. The ram, or lamb, was naturally linked to the newborn lambs of the season, and while in the Hired Man guise, the constellation was thought to represent the shepherd bringing in the barley harvest. Over time, and with the intervention of the Greeks, the name changed, and the lamb became the horned ram, synonymous with 'the Golden Fleece'.

To the ancient Egyptians, Aries was the god Amun Ra. A powerful deity with the body of a man and the head of a ram, he was a symbol of new life, fertility and growth, and associated with the coming of spring.

RITUAL TO BOOST ENTHUSIASM

This ritual can be performed at any time during the month of Aries. It will help you find focus and restore your enthusiasm, both characteristics attributed to this dynamic zodiac sign.

Daffodils, being a herald of spring, are closely associated with Aries, and they're the perfect bloom to use in this ritual.

You will need a bunch of daffodils, a vase and a pen or pencil and paper.

✴ Buy or pick a bunch of daffodils, and arrange the blooms in a vase filled with water.

✴ Spend a few minutes appreciating the daffodil. Consider the way it looks, and its sweet uplifting scent.

✴ Think about words that describe how the flower makes you feel, for example, 'positive', 'happy' or 'vibrant'. Now incorporate these words into a magical affirmation for yourself, such as, 'Every minute is an opportunity for me to feel positive, happy and vibrant.'

✴ Write the affirmation on the paper, fold it up, and place beneath the vase to encourage these attributes to grow.

✴ Every time you replenish the water in the vase, repeat the affirmation you have created.

RULING PLANET

MARS

The fiery red planet governs Aries, and just like the Roman god of war who shares its name, Mars brings attitude and sass. Born to Juno, the queen of the heavens and protector of Rome, Mars was conceived when the goddess ate a sacred flower gifted to her by the deity Flora, in a bid to produce a child without the help of her husband, Jupiter. The resulting babe burst forth from her womb, a wilful example of what can be achieved with inventiveness and bold determination, and was aptly named Mars, meaning 'man'.

Upon the battlefield Mars was in his element, charging forwards and creating chaos, often with little thought. A mighty warrior, he used his powers to instil courage into the Roman soldiers, and they looked to him for direction and protection. The planet is a representation of the god and the bloodshed that followed in his wake, and encapsulates all of his greatest qualities, being associated with dynamic action. Its influence upon this sign of the zodiac can be seen in the confidence and positivity of those born under its ruby red glare, and their ability to lead and inspire others.

PLANET RITUAL

RITUAL FOR CONFIDENCE

Tune in to the proactive, powerful energy of Mars with this simple breathing ritual, which combines a meditative exercise with a visualization. This can be carried out at any time during Aries season, and is particularly effective before a big event when you might need a confidence boost.

★ Sit on the floor with your back straight and your shoulders relaxed. If it helps, sit right up against a wall to support your back.

★ Place your hands with palms facing upwards on your lap in front of you.

★ Close your eyes, and visualize the red planet before you. See it as a giant, vivid ball of rosy light.

★ Draw a long slow breath in through your nose, and imagine that you are taking in some of that red energy.

★ Hold the breath for a moment and feel that energy sit in the centre of your chest fuelling your passion and warming your heart.

★ Release the breath slowly through your mouth and visualize your entire body encased in a glowing red aura.

★ Repeat this cycle of breathing. Imagine the vibrant energy of Mars infusing your body with every inhalation you take.

★ When you're ready, open your eyes, and give your limbs a gentle shake. You should feel strong and energized.

ARIES CHARACTER AND ATTRIBUTES

THE LEADER

As the first sign of the zodiac, supercharged rams are focused and full of enthusiasm. There's no time to spare when they have their eye on the prize. It's all about putting the best foot forwards and going for gold. It's no wonder so many of them excel at sports, and other competitive pastimes. Being a feisty fire sign, they're driven by passion and the will to succeed, and this motivates them in all things.

If you're in a relationship with an Aries, you'll know about it. The speed with which they sweep you off your feet will leave your head spinning. It's all or nothing for this impulsive sign. They feel things deeply, but this can also make them highly sensitive and quick to react when they feel slighted. Hot-headed is a phrase often associated with rambunctious rams, but while they may expect a lot of attention, they give more than their share back, being generous in heart, mind and energy. Effective and confident leaders, the ram is fearless and will jump straight into situations, often before thinking of the consequences. Some might say this is foolish, but to Aries it's a necessity. Why waste time? Life is short and these playful characters want to experience every bit of it.

TAURUS

APRIL 20TH TO MAY 20TH

CONSTELLATION DESCRIPTION

TAURUS THE BULL

Best Time to View: January

Part of a cluster of stars called the Hyades, the constellation of Taurus the bull creates a V shaped pattern in the night sky as it charges full pelt towards the constellation of Orion the hunter. The star-studded frame outlines the shape of the bull's face, and is complemented by Aldebaran (the eye of the bull), a blazing red star around seventy light years away. Much brighter than our own sun, this old star is quite the feature of the constellation. That said, it still commands the bull's features and hints at the power behind this sturdy beast.

CONSTELLATION MYTH

THE WHITE BULL

It's no surprise that the Greek myth behind this constellation has love at its heart. According to the tale, the Phoenician princess Europa was the most stunning beauty to ever walk the Earth, and had caught the eye of the king of the gods, Zeus. Though Zeus had had many illicit affairs, Europa's purity and lightness of being intoxicated him with passion. So he devised a plan to make her his own. Disguising his godly status, he appeared in the form of a white bull, with huge golden horns and eyes like the liquid dark seas. Europa was instantly smitten with the creature, and so Zeus seized his chance, and lifted her up onto his back, and into the air.

Across the skies they flew until they eventually reached the shores of Crete, and it was here that Zeus revealed his true nature and his intentions, wooing the princess with promises of love and many gifts. Among his tokens of affection were the bronze giant Talos, to guard and protect the princess, and the hunting dog Laelaps. Eventually, Zeus' efforts paid off, and they were wed. Although Europa gave Zeus three sons, who became the leaders of the Underworld, their marriage didn't last. The princess went on to remarry King Asterius, thus becoming the queen of Crete.

In honour of their relationship, and perhaps because of the sons she had given him, Zeus decided to create a permanent reminder of the love they had shared, by turning the bull form into a heavenly starscape, and the constellation Taurus.

FOLKLORE FROM AROUND THE WORLD

WATCHER OF THE HEAVENS

Being one of the oldest constellations, Taurus has many stories and snippets of folklore associated with it. To the ancient Babylonians it was known as 'the Heavenly Bull', or sometimes the 'Bull of Heaven', a creature synonymous with strength and fertility. This bull was a plundering destructive creature sent by the goddess Ishtar, and was eventually killed by the Mesopotamian character Gilgamesh. The constellation Orion represents the hero about to slay the bull.

To the ancient Egyptians, Taurus was a symbol of the coming of spring. The Inuit people know the constellation as 'Nanook', meaning 'the spirit of the polar bear', with the remaining stars in Hyades as wild dogs, keeping the creature at bay. In ancient Persia, Aldebaran, the brightest star and the eye of the bull, was revered as one of the four royal stars and called 'the watcher of the eastern sky'.

RITUAL TO CONNECT WITH THE NATURAL WORLD

This ritual can be done at any point while the Sun is in the sign of Taurus, and can be incorporated into your daily schedule. By reaffirming your connection with nature, you tap in to the strength and resilience of this earth sign.

★ You're going to go on a mindful walk; it doesn't have to be long. This ritual is about engaging with the natural world, so choose somewhere with lots of green space.

★ Take your time; place your feet firmly on the ground as you walk and feel the steadying influence of the earth.

★ Imagine that every breath imbues you with energy, and feel the earth's power being drawn up through the soles of your feet and into your chest.

★ First, think about what you can see, from the vibrant, fresh greenery to the colour of the skies.

★ Next, think about what you can hear, such as birds chirruping in the distance, or the rustling, snuffling sounds of woodland creatures.

★ Notice what you feel, paying attention to the breeze as it grazes your skin. Reach out and touch the bark of a tree. How does it feel?

★ Finally, think about what you can smell and taste. Notice the freshness of the air, or the sweet dampness of the soil. Enjoy every aspect of the walk, and notice how it recharges body, mind and spirit.

VENUS

The planet Venus, like the Roman goddess of the same name, is associated with love and beauty, and governs Taurus, sign of the bull. This might seem like a juxtaposition, but in fact makes perfect sense. The bull is a passionate land dweller, staying close to the earth and guided by its senses. It delights in the warmth of the Sun and the touch of the grass beneath its feet. The sensual influence of Venus meets the earthy sensibilities of the bull to create a pleasure-seeking, passionate sign that craves love and stability.

In her guise as the Roman goddess, Venus enjoyed dabbling in the affairs of men. She loved to be the centre of attention, both to satisfy her ego and for the reassurance of being adored. Tales of her romantic exploits are well-known, and her passionate affairs brought her security and satisfaction. This same urge drives the bull, who also longs for the security of a loving relationship. Born from the sea spray created when her father Uranus' genitals were tossed in the ocean, Venus emerged fully grown and ready for action. Unlike her Greek counterpart Aphrodite, Venus dabbled in affairs of the state, and influenced protection, finances and fertility, along with her more usual associations of love, beauty and desire.

RITUAL FOR SELF-LOVE

Tap into the loving energy of Venus, and give yourself some gentle self-care with this pampering ritual. Perform this exercise on any Friday (the day associated with the goddess Venus), during the Taurus month.

You will need lavender essential oil and a carrier oil such as almond or olive oil.

★ Add a couple of drops of lavender essential oil, which is renowned for its soothing properties, to a tablespoon of carrier oil such as almond or olive oil, and mix well.

★ Massage a drop of the mixture gently into each hand. As you do this, think about all of the lovely things your hands do for you, and how they help you nurture and care for yourself and others. Consider how they help you create things, whether cooking a tasty meal, writing a poem, crafting or making your home a cosy space.

★ Continue by thinking about your body as a whole, and all the beautiful things it has done for you.

★ Acknowledge your body's importance and say, 'I am made of love. I am love. I love myself.'

TAURUS CHARACTER AND ATTRIBUTES

THE TENACIOUS

Steadfast and loyal, the devoted bull is a big softy at heart, and a huge fan of romance. These earthy characters love the pleasures of life. From a delicious homecooked meal to a scented candlelit bath, they can't get enough of the good stuff, and are one of the most sensual zodiac signs. Sentimental bulls will go above and beyond for the ones they love, to the point of putting up with bad behaviour. They are incredibly devoted and loyal in relationships, and tend to only see the best in their partners. They can hold their own in argument, but they prefer to quietly sidestep confrontations in the first place. The tenacious Taurus is forever hopeful and will hang in there till the end in the belief that all will be well. That said, push them too far and the bull will charge, and when that happens, you'll need more than a red flag to distract them!

Bulls can be stubborn, being a fixed earth sign, but the flip side of this is unerring determination that will take these characters to the top. Being a creative force of nature, it's no surprise that many Taureans become world leaders in their field of choice. While other signs might give up at the first, second or third hurdle, the focused bull will draw upon inner reserves of strength, and continue to strive and thrive. Stability is important to this sign, so once they have reached their goals, they'll aim for a pleasant, no-stress environment and a routine that suits their temperament.

GEMINI

MAY 21ST TO JUNE 20TH

GEMINI THE TWINS

Best Time to View: February

Floating in the Northern Hemisphere, two bright stars connected by a seemingly invisible thread of light hold the thirtieth largest constellation together, Gemini the twins. The twins are bound by two parallel lines of stars, and at the head of each one a dazzling star represents Castor and Pollux, or Polydeuces as he was known in Greek mythology. The fated twins hang in the sky and are clearly visible during the winter months. While Pollux is the brighter of the two, Castor is actually made up of a tight cluster of stars that appear as one star.

TWO HALVES OF ONE SOUL

The Greek myth that shaped the constellation Gemini may at first glance appear to be a tragic tale, but the essence of the narrative celebrates unity; it is the story of two souls born together of different fathers, but forever entwined.

The queen of Sparta gave birth to a set of twins, Castor, the son of the mortal king Tyndareus, and Polydeuces, a magical gift from a brief fling with the king of the gods Zeus. The parentage of both mattered little to the boys who grew up together and were the best of friends. Gifted with strength and dexterity, they became known as 'the Dioscuri', a fighting duo that were hard to beat. Wherever they went adoring fans followed, and they even joined Jason and his Argonauts on their mission to claim the Golden Fleece, being such accomplished warriors.

While the boys enjoyed many exploits together, Polydeuces, being immortal, always promised to look after his brother Castor and be there for him. After all, they had come into the world together and nothing could separate them. But unfortunately death could not be slighted, and would eventually drive a wedge between the two. In a fated skirmish with another set of twins, Castor was killed. Polydeuces was beside himself with grief, and lay holding his brother in his hands. Looking up to the heavens, he pleaded with his father Zeus to let him die so that he could be with his brother. The god did not want to give up his son to the Underworld, so instead he lifted both brothers into the sky, transforming them into the twinkling twins and the constellation of Gemini. In this way, they would be remembered, and could remain together for eternity.

FOLKLORE FROM AROUND THE WORLD

THE GREAT TWINS

The Babylonians also embraced the dual aspect of the twins from the Gemini constellation. They called this star grouping 'the Great Twins', and gave each star a name. One was called Meshlamtaea and the other Lugalirr, and they were thought to be two different aspects of the king of the Underworld, Nergal, who was also the god of plague and pestilence. It was thought that one of the twins would travel back and forth to the Underworld in a messenger role, and that together, the two aspects of the king were guardians of the summertime entrance to the realm of the dead.

RITUAL FOR BALANCE AND UNITY

This ritual can be carried out at any time when the Sun is in the sign of Gemini. It will help you unite the different aspects of your personality, and provide a sense of balance and wholeness. If you're feeling vulnerable, or at odds with yourself, this ritual can help to bring clarity and confidence.

You will need a handful of tealights and matches or a lighter.

★ Arrange the tealights in a pattern to represent the constellation Gemini. Start by creating two parallel lines of tealights, then cap these lines together at the top with two more tealights to create an arch.

★ Light the candles, and sit for a moment.

★ Let your thoughts flow in and out of your mind, and don't try and control them. Simply focus on your breathing and the gentle rise and fall of your chest.

★ Place both hands over your heart and say, 'Like the stars in a constellation, I am made of many things, all of which work together to create me, myself and I.'

★ Inhale deeply and as you exhale say, 'I am united, at one and balanced.' Then blow out the candles.

RULING PLANET

MERCURY

Mercury may be the smallest planet in the Solar System, but what it lacks in size it makes up for in speed. This nifty mover orbits the Sun, completing three circular journeys per one Earth year. It's what you would expect from the planet of movement, change and communication, and goes some way to explain its influence upon the zodiac sign Gemini. No wonder those born under this sun sign are so quick-witted!

The Romans recognized that this was the planet of movement, and the corresponding god of myth and legend, Mercury, was fleet-footed and mercurial to match. Recognized as the god of commerce, trade and communication, Mercury was also something of a trickster and enjoyed playing pranks on gods and humans. While most of the deities preferred to keep their distance from the people of Earth, Mercury enjoyed mixing with humankind and would often disguise his true nature in order to mingle. In his role as a messenger god, Mercury would travel between heaven and Earth and pass on information, but he couldn't resist throwing a spanner in the works occasionally, just to see how people would react.

Mercury's natural curiosity and nimble ways can clearly be seen in the mental dexterity of those born under the sign of Gemini, and the way they navigate the world around them.

PLANET RITUAL

RITUAL FOR FLEXIBILITY
AND ADAPTABILITY

Mercury is all about communication and movement. As a planet it is changeable, able to adapt swiftly by moving into retrograde, and then back again should the situation require. Embrace this flexible energy using movement and positive thought to bring it into your own life, so that you can adapt and seize opportunities when they are presented to you.

★ Position your feet so that they are wide apart, and you feel a stretch travelling up your inner thighs.

★ Hold your arms out to the sides, at shoulder level.

★ Take a long breath in and as you exhale begin to twist at the waist, from side to side.

★ Imagine you're creating a wide circle with your hands.

★ Continue breathing deeply as you spin, and each time try and stretch a little further to make the circle complete.

★ Think of yourself as a small planet spinning on the spot.

★ Feel the energy you are creating with this movement, and how it makes you feel alive. Notice how your body responds and seems to become more flexible with every twist.

★ Slowly reduce the pace of your spinning, until you are standing still. Bring your arms to your sides and relax.

GEMINI CHARACTER AND ATTRIBUTES

THE SOCIAL BUTTERFLY

Forever moving forwards, the Gemini character is in a constant search for stimulation, whether that's intellectual, or in one-to-one relationships. These gregarious souls adore learning about the world around them and communicating with others. Fast thinking and equally quick witted, they love to engage in a verbal exchange, particularly if it challenges their mercurial brain. There's a playful side to these social butterflies, and any time spent in their company is a joy, but they can also be serious and even maudlin at times, and tend to flip between the two sides of their personality. It can be hard to get a handle on a Gemini because they change so swiftly, and they themselves will often admit to feeling restless without knowing why.

Finding love can be something of a mission for the typical Gemini. While they enjoy the thrill of the chase and meeting new people, they easily lose interest if their potential beau does not pique their interest beyond the physical. For this air sign it's all about the brain, and effortless communication is key to any relationship. Being so inquisitive, Geminis are ideally suited to careers and pastimes that allow them to dig deep, and ask lots of questions. It's no wonder they can appear nosy at times. In truth they're just genuinely interested in the world around them. After all, knowledge is power when it comes to the sign of the twins.

SUMMER

As the heady months of summer swoop in, they bring long lazy days with light-filled vistas and a brightness that stretches over space and time. The bountiful landscape is a riot of colour, and flowers reach to the heavens, their petals praising the shimmering beauty of the skies. At night, the sky responds with its own glorious performance, and while the nights may be shorter, there is much to enjoy here.

As the constellations of Gemini and Cancer bow down over the western horizon, Libra's scales emerge to balance the picture. Look just south of the ecliptic and you will spot Sagittarius the archer in his famous stance. Recognizable for its teapot-like formation, this constellation is home to a number of deep space objects, including dwarf galaxies. As constellation Orion sets in the west, you will see Scorpius rising in the east. One of the most prominent constellations at this time of year, the twinkling, J-shaped outline of the scorpion is hard to miss, thanks to the fiery red heart star Antares, which can be viewed with the naked eye.

With the sun at its prime, so the zodiac signs roll onwards; Cancer the crab skitters across the sky to make way for Leo's lordly roar, until finally Virgo the maiden steps gently out to take centre stage in the last of the summer months.

CANCER

JUNE 21ST TO JULY 22ND

CANCER THE CRAB

Best Time to View: March

First catalogued by the Greek astronomer Ptolemy in the 2nd century AD, Cancer, also called 'the Celestial Crab', is almost impossible to see with the naked eye. Delicate like the sign it governs, Cancer is a medium-sized constellation, with a group of stars at its centre called the beehive cluster. This too appears faint, like a gossamer cloud floating inside the Y-shaped frame of the crab. Its brightest star is Al Tarf, sometimes called Beta Cancri, 290 light years from the Earth.

THE GATEWAY TO EARTH

Known as 'the Gate of Men', Cancer the crab with its barely-there appearance could have been dismissed for its lack of size and sparkle, but the Greeks recognized the power of this constellation, imbuing it with meaning. To them, it was the starry portal through which souls seeking life upon the Earth had to pass; before being born, each soul had to first slip through the gates of the realm of Cancer. The legend of how it became so is a story of love, jealousy and one sea creature's devotion to its mistress.

Karkinos the crab was most likely minding his own business on the shoreline when the goddess Hera summoned him. Besieged with jealousy after years of watching her husband Zeus cavort with other women, Hera took her rage out upon Zeus' illegitimate son, the demigod Heracles, a powerful hero who was adored by the people. Hera cast a terrible curse upon him which left him plagued by demons. In a fit of anguish, he killed his wife and family, and as punishment for this, the gods decreed he complete twelve deadly labours.

One of these labours saw Heracles going head-to-head with the mighty Hydra, a monstrous nine-headed serpent. Each time one of its heads was cut off, a new one grew back in its place. Hera, leaving nothing to chance, summoned Karkinos to assist by distracting the hero from the fight. The crab, faithful to the goddess and feisty, nipped at Heracles' heels and tried courageously to wound him, but it was a futile task. In the end, Heracles crushed the crab's shell underfoot, and managed to defeat the Hydra by burning each severed neck so that the serpent could not regenerate. Hera, feeling remorseful for the part she had played in the crab's death, decided to honour the creature. She lifted its tiny form into the sky, and transformed it into a cluster of stars. And so the constellation Cancer found new life as the gateway to Earth.

FOLKLORE FROM AROUND THE WORLD

THE SHELLED ONE

In Babylonia, this constellation was thought to represent a tortoise, and was sometimes referred to as the 'Seat of Anu', a Mesopotamian sky god predominant at the time. The shell-like shape was also acknowledged in ancient Egypt, where it was believed to be a scarab, a type of dung beetle. This was a sacred symbol to the ancient Egyptians, seen as an emblem of immortality and the regeneration of the Sun.

In Chinese astronomy the constellation belongs to four 'lunar mansions', segments of the ecliptic where the

Moon passes during its orbit. These mansions are located in a part of the universe known as the Vermilion Bird of the South, which is associated with fire and the season of summer.

RITUAL TO RELEASE THE PAST

This ritual, which embodies the intuitive, receptive qualities of this zodiac sign, will help you harness the power of Cancer during this month. It's particularly useful if you're feeling sensitive or emotional, as it can help you release the past and be open to the ebb and flow of life's journey. This ritual works with the element of water that governs this sign, so you will need to find a free-flowing body of water, like a river, stream, lake or even the sea.

You will need a white flower head of your choice.

★ Head to a body of water and take a white flower head with you to symbolize the illuminative power of the Moon.

★ Stand at the water's edge with the flower in your hands, and close your eyes for a moment. Listen to the sound of the water lapping at your feet.

★ Hold the flower close to your heart and imagine that any pain, anxiety or fear for the future is being absorbed by the petals. Breathe deeply and take your time.

★ Gradually open your eyes, inhale deeply, and as you release the breath, drop the flower into the water.

★ Watch it being carried away, and know that any pain, guilt or worry is flowing from you, and you are free to open your heart to new experiences and opportunities.

RULING PLANET

MOON

Unlike most of the zodiac, Cancer is not ruled by a planet, and instead claims the Moon as its mentor. This goes some way to explain the ebb and flow of Cancerian moods, and the deeply intense thought processes they're blessed with. Just as the Earth's natural satellite influences the tides, it is also connected to the inner workings of the mind, and the sensitivity with which we experience the world around us.

The Moon is associated with intuition and creativity, and has a mystical energy that gives it an almost otherworldly feel. Indeed, people born under this sign can appear not of this world at times, because they have a tendency to distance themselves, and shift in shape and form like this luminescent orb. The Moon is revered around the world and continues to maintain its enigmatic allure, something which can also be said for sensitive Cancerians.

To the Romans, the Moon was the goddess Luna, a beautiful being, and the sister of Sol, the Sun god, and Aurora, the goddess of the dawn. Unlike her more proactive siblings, Luna's delicate light was a thing of mystery and as such, any tales relating to her were filled with enchantment. According to myth, she embarked on an affair with a handsome shepherd called Endymion who had also caught the eye of the king of the gods Jupiter. He had bestowed Endymion with the gift of eternal life and sleep, but this didn't deter Luna who was so enamoured she visited him nightly, bathing him in the loving glow of her protection. Together they had fifty children, known as 'the Menae'.

RITUAL TO BOOST PSYCHIC CONNECTION

The Moon's mystical energy is healing and uplifting, and can help us connect more deeply with our intuition. Use this ritual on a Monday, the day connected to the Moon, and it will help you harness its psychic power during Cancer season.

You will need a white candle to represent the Moon, and matches or a lighter.

★ Light your candle and place it in your window.

★ If you can see the Moon, take a moment to consider its presence, its current shape, and how it makes you feel.

★ Close your eyes, and as you exhale, throw your arms open wide as if embracing the Moon's light.

★ As you inhale, bring your hands together in front of you, palms together, and then push inwards towards your chest, as if drawing in the Moon's energy.

★ Repeat this exercise at least three times, feeling the power of the Moon's energy lighting you up from the inside.

★ Let the candle burn down in quiet contemplation.

THE PSYCHIC

Cancerians may be emotionally led, but that doesn't mean there isn't an inherent well of strength lurking within them. As you might expect from a water sign, these ethereal beauties have hidden depths which they don't reveal to just anyone. It takes time, work and trust to crack the average Cancerian shell and get to the heart of the matter, but it's worth the effort. This sign may appear secretive and sometimes aloof, but it's actually a protective mechanism they've developed over time to shield them from hurt.

Deeply intuitive, the clever crab is tuned in at all levels, and able to read the room and detect atmospheres most might miss. Often gifted with psychic abilities, this sign is instinctive, trusting what they feel, rather than what they hear or see upon the surface. In relationships, they're sensitive and caring, but this can come across as controlling at times. That said, they will go the extra mile for family and friends, particularly in times of crisis. Home is important to the crab, and they will do their best to make a cosy, safe environment for those they love. Once you have established a bond with a Cancerian, it's very hard to break. They will go to the ends of the Earth to protect those they love, and should you slight one, be prepared for some passive-aggressive exchanges and the odd pincer nip.

LEO

JULY 23ᴿᴰ TO AUGUST 22ᴺᴰ

LEO THE LION

Best Time to View: April

The twelfth largest constellation in the night sky, Leo the lion is perhaps the most recognizable, thanks to its defined shape. The head of the beast – which resembles a back-to-front question mark formed of a group of stars known as the sickle – moves fluidly into the main body to create a lion, crouched and ready to pounce. Containing the Leo Triplet – a collection of three galaxies – and the blue-white star Regulus, the brightest in this constellation, Leo commands the skies and cements his role as a celestial protector.

CONSTELLATION MYTH

THE NEMEAN LION

There's a reason why the constellation of Leo stands so powerfully in the night sky. After all, the lion it represents was a worthy adversary and imbued with supernatural strength.

According to Greek legend, the constellation is based on the Nemean Lion, a terrifying, magical beast with a hide so tough it could withstand any weapon. This mystical creature has murky origins. Some thought it was the offspring of Echidna, a half-woman, half-snake being, and her partner Typhon, a hideous monster, while other stories suggest the lion was the result of a coupling between Zeus and the Moon goddess Selene. Some tales suggest that it was the goddess Hera who'd had a hand in the lion's creation, and that she planned to use him to destroy Zeus. Either way, the creature had powers that meant it was virtually undefeatable, and because of this, could do anything it wanted.

Devastating the Nemean landscape, it plundered through nearby villages, killing the inhabitants and kidnapping young women, carrying them away to its cave lair. The gods, who preferred to keep their distance from the human realm, could see the havoc the beast had caused and decided to pit the hero Heracles against the lion as part of his twelve deadly labours. As the creature was impervious to spear or blade, Heracles soon realized he would need brute force to kill him. In the end, he strangled the lion with his bare hands.

Hera, who had been watching the events from the heavens, was crushed by the loss of the lion, and valued the courage and strength it had shown during its life. As a reward for this, and to commemorate the magical beast, she cast him into the sky as the grouping of stars known as Leo the lion – beautiful, commanding and forever vibrant.

FOLKLORE FROM AROUND THE WORLD

THE BIG CAT

It's thought that the Mesopotamians had a lion constellation as early as 4000 BC, and the big cat was often used as a symbol of power. The four constellations of the Lion, the Bull, the Scorpion and The Great One (Aquarius) were thought to be the four cardinal points in the yearly calendar, relating to the spring equinox, summer solstice, autumn equinox and the winter solstice. Babylonian astronomers recorded the constellation as UR.GU.LA, meaning 'The Great Lion', and associated it with Ishtar, the goddess of love, war and fertility.

To the ancient Egyptians, the Leo constellation represented the watchful eye of Sekhmet, the lion-headed goddess of war. This ferocious feline deity was also associated with protection and strength.

LEO RITUAL

RITUAL FOR COURAGE AND CONFIDENCE

This ritual employs a simple but powerful visualization, and will help you tap into the courage and confidence of this sign. You can perform it at any time during the month of Leo.

★ The Nemean Lion was protected by skin that could not be pierced. While you may not come to blows with spears or swords, words and negative energy can affect how you feel and penetrate your aura, zapping your confidence. To prevent this and give yourself a boost, visualize your entire body encased in golden light. Imagine this light is a shield which keeps negative energy at bay.

★ Place a hand over your heart, and press lightly as you inhale. Imagine you're pressing a button which boosts the light of your aura, causing it to glow vibrantly.

★ As you exhale, visualize your energy field extending outwards.

★ Repeat at any point during the day when you need to feel strong and confident.

RULING PLANET

SUN

Vivacious Leo is unique among the signs in being governed by a star – the Sun. Associated with joy, confidence and vitality, this fiery ball of energy has been the subject of fascination since the dawn of humanity. Mythologies throughout the world have done their best to explain its journey through the sky with adventurous narratives. The ancient Egyptians believed that the Sun god Ra carried this ball of light through the air upon his chariot, while being chased by the demon serpent Apep. The Norse people believed in the goddess Sunna, who would ride through the sky on her chariot pursued by the wolf Fenrir. On occasion he would get so close that he could snatch a bite, causing an eclipse. To the Romans, the Sun was Sol, a powerful god who protected the empire, and was worshipped by a cult of followers.

The Sun's influence is mighty, and never more so than with Leo, the sign it governs. Like the Sun, orbited by the planets in the Solar System, those born under Leo have an inherent need to be the centre of attention. The Sun's shine cannot be ignored or dimmed, and Leos exude warmth and confidence. The Sun never goes into retrograde, and remains a constant, consistent presence at all times, just as Leo remains steadfastly devoted and loyal to loved ones.

PLANET RITUAL

RITUAL FOR STRENGTH AND HEALING

This energizing ritual helps you harness the power and vitality of the Sun's rays, and can be used to harness this warmth for healing, strength and wellbeing. You can practise this ritual at any point during Leo season, and it works especially well on sunny days, when you can feel the sunlight upon your face, and also on a Sunday, the day corresponding to the Sun.

★ Stand outside in a sunny spot. Drop your weight down slightly into your lower legs and feel the connection that you have with the earth.

★ Close your eyes and draw your attention to the top of your head. Feel the warmth of the Sun hitting the centre of your scalp.

★ Imagine the rays like streaks of golden light that seep beneath your skin.

★ As you breathe in, imagine drawing that light down through your head, and feel it sit behind your eyes.

★ Let it rest here for a moment and feel the gentle warmth soothe your mind.

★ With each breath, imagine drawing the Sun's energy further into your body, along your neck and throat and into your chest. Feel it warm your heart, and fill your stomach. Feel the muscles of your body relax into the heat.

★ Breathe deeply and enjoy the vibrant healing sensations, as you bathe in the Sun's glory.

THE ENTERTAINER

Leos are fire signs and love to languish in the heat of the limelight. It's their favourite place, and contrary to popular belief, it's not because they're self-obsessed. In truth, they enjoy entertaining others, and while they crave attention, they also like to return the favour and make other people feel special. It's all about give and take, and this pussycat likes to create a fuss. Whether they're looking for adoration, a burning new passion or just to share the love, they radiate sunshine wherever they go.

Confident and sometimes outspoken, Leos tend to make good leaders because they like to take control of a situation, and don't mind being at the heart of the action, even when that comes with consequences. If anyone's going to stir up trouble, it's this cat. They're quite happy to be controversial, plonking their big paws where they shouldn't. That said, they're hugely protective too, especially of their loved ones. Bravery is the main quality associated with these characters, and they're not afraid to stand up for what they believe in, even when the going gets tough.

Ego is the main issue when it comes to the lion, for while they enjoy seeing those they care about do well, they can sometimes get a touch of the green-eyed monster should the spotlight shift away from them. Leos love to be in love. They're extremely passionate and dedicated to their other half, and can be playful when it comes to romance. They also like a bit of drama in a relationship to spice things up, so it won't be plain sailing all the way. But it will always be interesting, fiery and full of fun!

VIRGO

AUGUST 23RD TO SEPTEMBER 22ND

CONSTELLATION DESCRIPTION

VIRGO THE MAIDEN

Best Time to View: May

The second largest constellation in the night sky, and the largest within the zodiac grouping, Virgo appears faint to the naked eye with one exception: the bright blue-white star Spica. This glimmering beauty is actually made up of two stars in a constant gravitational dance, and forms the stalk of wheat held by Virgo, the goddess of the harvest. The constellation also contains the Virgo Cluster, a collection of over 1,300 galaxies. This galaxy cluster is around sixty million light years away, and its proximity to the Local Cluster, which houses the Milky Way, means that the two move in unison, thanks to a strong gravitational pull.

CONSTELLATION MYTH

GODDESS OF THE UNDERWORLD

One Greek myth associated with Virgo attempts to explain its appearance in the skies of the Northern Hemisphere during late spring, and its apparent absence in autumn and winter.

In this story, the maiden Virgo represents Persephone, the beautiful daughter of Demeter, goddess of the harvest, who was kidnapped by the god of the Underworld, Hades. Persephone's mother was heartbroken at the loss of her daughter, and trailed the Earth and the heavens in search of her. She abandoned her role, causing the crops to fail and the people to suffer from this loss. Zeus, who was well aware of Persephone's fate and location, decided to intervene, requesting that Hades return the girl to her mother. But there were certain rules in the Underworld, the most important being that anyone who ate food from the Underworld would be tied to the realm forever. Hades, obsessed and desperate to keep hold of Persephone, encouraged her to eat the seeds of a pomegranate. For each of the six seeds she had consumed Persephone would have to spend six months of the year in the Underworld, and the remaining six would be spent with her mother, Demeter, in her rightful place.

Persephone's yearly return to her home, and with it the arrival of spring, coincides perfectly with the reappearance of the constellation Virgo in the skies of the Northern Hemisphere. The Sun also appears in this constellation during late summer, when farmers begin their harvest, so it makes perfect sense that Virgo was associated with the earthy goddess of the grain.

FOLKLORE FROM AROUND THE WORLD

THE HARVEST MAIDEN

Virgo, being a key constellation, takes many forms around the world. The Babylonians believed she was the goddess Ishtar, who, during her absence from the skies, searched the Underworld for her husband Tammuz. In Hindu mythology, Virgo is Kauni the maiden, while the Persians called her Khosha, 'the ear of wheat'. To the Hebrews, Virgo was Bethulah, meaning 'abundance in harvest'.

An alternative Greek myth depicts Virgo as the beautiful star maiden Astraea, goddess of purity and innocence. When all the gods finally left Earth to live in the heavens permanently, Astraea was the last to flee. She loved the Earth and its people, and found it hard to leave her post, but eventually was driven away by the lawless nature of humankind. She represents the earthy fixed nature of Virgo the virgin.

VIRGO RITUAL

RITUAL FOR CREATIVITY

This ritual taps into the resourceful, analytical qualities of Virgo, and can help if you have a particular issue or problem to solve. It can be done at any time when the Sun is in Virgo.

You will need a pen and paper.

★ Take a pen and some paper and draw a series of boxes, like a storyboard across the page.

★ In the first box, draw an image or symbol to represent a problem, and beneath it, write a sentence that sums it up.

★ Go to the box at the end of the strip, and draw a symbol or image to represent the best outcome to this problem, and write a sentence to describe this.

★ Now look at the boxes in-between, and think about the steps that you can take to reach this outcome. Be creative; fill in the boxes with any ideas that spring to mind. You can create multiple storyboards, and come up with alternative solutions to help you organize your thoughts. Doing something practical that allows you to be objective will help you see the potential options you have, and tap into the Virgo problem-solving mindset.

RULING PLANET

MERCURY

Mercury, both the planet and the Roman god of the same name, is associated with playfulness and communication, but it does have a serious methodical side, and it is this that influences the Virgo mind. As a trickster character in Roman mythology, Mercury would perform social experiments, engaging with humans in disguise to find out how they would react in certain situations. He would assimilate all of the details, and then form his opinion. As such he was organized in his ventures, and often went to Earth on fact-finding missions. Tales abound of him disguising himself as a homeless beggar to see who might help, and offer a morsel of food. While most townsfolk ignored his pleas, there was always one individual who would go out of their way to offer assistance, proving Mercury's theories that humans could be both good and bad.

The methodical, analytical qualities of Mercury can be seen in the sun sign Virgo. Being the planet of commerce and trade, Mercury also encourages routine and introspection, which are just as important when it comes to communication and successful endeavours.

PLANET RITUAL

RITUAL FOR INNER REFLECTION

Turn inwards, reflect and assimilate your skills by using the methodical influence of the planet Mercury. This gentle ritual can be carried out at any time when the Sun is in Virgo, but works particularly well as a mid-week reflection to help you feel motivated (Wednesday is Mercury's day, so is the perfect time to practise this ritual).

You will need a candle, matches or a lighter and a journal and pen.

★ Light a candle to create a soothing atmosphere, and sit with a journal and pen.

★ Consider how you feel right now, and where you are in your life. Think about all of things that you have achieved, from small goals, to bigger life changes. Make a list of these accomplishments.

★ Consider all the skills that you have used to reach each one of these goals. If you're struggling to think of anything, reflect upon your week and any smaller accomplishments, and how you achieved them. What qualities did you need to spur you on? Write down whatever comes to mind.

★ Look at the two lists you have created. You will see a picture forming and you'll be able to see all of the skills and talents at your disposal. Be proud of where you are, and know that each experience is a lesson that you can draw upon in the future.

★ Re-read the lists at any point during the Virgo season, and acknowledge your amazing skillset.

VIRGO CHARACTER AND ATTRIBUTES

THE INTELLECTUAL

Virgos are gentle characters who will go out of their way to help others; from well thought out advice to practical help dispensed with plenty of muscle, nothing is too much trouble for this sun sign. They enjoy working as part of team, and like to think they're indispensable, which for the most part they are. Virgos are perfectionists, so everything they do will be to the highest standard, and they expect the same from others.

Methodical and hardworking, the Virgo mind is like a computer making sense of information, and creating order out of chaos. Being an earth sign, they're quite fixed in their approach to life, and their opinions will be formed through careful analysis. Friendly and warm, Virgos are diligent companions and partners, and are likely to show affection by the things they do rather than any ostentatious displays of affection. If you're expecting romance then it's probably the last thing on the table, but if you want someone to rely on, particularly in times of trouble, then this is the sign to go for. Quick-witted and intellectual, Virgos can on occasion be judgemental of others, but while they may appear to be nit-picking, they're most critical of themselves. These resourceful characters only want the best for themselves and for those they care for.

AUTUMN

The veil of autumn may mute some of summer's brightness, but it has its own burnished glow. Slowly, steadily, the world turns inwards. The plants and flowers curl their heads towards the earth, and the leaves ripen and fall, their gold and bronze hues carpeting the ground. Animals find warmth in nooks and crannies, and begin their preparations for the winter, and we take refuge in our homes, lighting candles and fires as the nights draw in.

Above our heads, the celestial realm is shifting, as summer's constellations begin their gradual descent to the west. In the east, new stars are rising, and while the night skies may not be as clear, the constellations that grace them are vivid. Capricornus the goat peeps over the southern horizon, while Aquarius the water bearer's size alone makes it easy to pinpoint. Bordering this giant, you'll find the fainter Pisces the fish, and Aries, whose ram's horns are marked by the bright yellow star Hamal.

Among the riot of changes introduced by the new season are three more zodiac signs as the calendar shifts. First Libra, the scales of reason, and close behind crawls Scorpio, with its stinging tail. Finally the archer rides into view, with Sagittarius being the last star sign of the Autumn months.

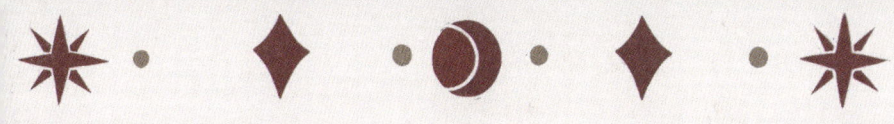

LIBRA

SEPTEMBER 23RD TO OCTOBER 22ND

LIBRA THE SCALES

Best Time to View: June

While this constellation may be faint and almost spectral
against the backdrop of the sky, it plays an important role.
This is thanks to the Sun passing over its surface during
the autumn equinox, when day and night are equal. It's
no wonder that Libra the scales is associated with balance
and harmony. The Libra constellation is home to one of the
most fascinating stars, Methuselah, which when it was first
discovered, was believed to be sixteen billion years old, a
figure which exceeds the creation of the universe. Since
then, astronomers have re-calculated this figure, which
now stands at just under fourteen and a half billion years.

CONSTELLATION MYTH

THE SCALES OF JUSTICE

Libra is the only constellation associated with an object
rather than an animal or a person, but the scales of justice
that represent Libra are linked to the Greek goddess Themis.

Beautiful and fair, Themis was the consort of Zeus for a time.
Sitting at his right hand, holding her scales of justice aloft,
she was the epitome of fairness. Calm and imbued with a
sense of balance, Themis soon became important in the
decision-making process of the pantheon, and Zeus would
often confide in her when he had a problem. Because of
this, she was known as the 'Lady of Good Counsel', and even
after Zeus had moved on to another love, he kept Themis at
his side for her wisdom and objective point of view.

Also associated with prophecy, Themis was a popular goddess with the people, and in time they built the stone temple at Delphi in her honour. According to legend, it was there that she sat holding court with her scales of justice in one hand. Those who sought a resolution or advice for the future would petition her for help. Like her daughter Astraea, who is associated with the zodiac sign Virgo, she too decided to stay behind when the gods fled the Earth. Her role as mediator and dispenser of justice was more important to her, and so she set up home at Delphi and continued to advise humankind on legal matters. It was thought that she was integral in setting up and creating the justice system, and as a thank you for her dedicated service, a constellation of stars known as Libra was mapped in her honour.

FOLKLORE FROM AROUND THE WORLD

THE BALANCE OF HEAVEN

The Babylonians were the first to associate Libra with balance. Their astronomers noticed the way the Sun shone upon the constellation at the time of the autumn equinox. They called the star grouping ZIB.BA.AN.NA, meaning 'the balance of heaven', and linked it with the Sun god Shamash. This ancient Mesopotamian deity also governed justice and truth and was called upon to issue judgement. It was thought he had the all-seeing eye, and knew the truth of all deeds, and his role was to weigh up evidence fairly during disputes.

The ancient Egyptians also equated Libra with their goddess of justice Ma'at. It was her responsibility to weigh the heart of a recently deceased person against her 'feather of truth'. If heart and feather were in balance, then the soul could continue its journey on to the afterlife.

LIBRA RITUAL

RITUAL FOR GRATITUDE

Librans love to surround themselves with beautiful things, and they acknowledge when something gives them pleasure. This mindful ritual will help you engage with your surroundings and recognize the magic in your own life. It can be carried out at any point when the Sun is in Libra.

★ Take a moment at any point during your day to stop and look around you. Pick out one thing that catches your eye. It could be something beautiful like a flower in a garden, or more functional like your favourite chair or mug.

★ Hone in on this one item, and notice everything about it. Look at the size and shape, the colour and design, and think about what it is made of, and how it was made or formed. Does it have a scent, or a sound associated with it? Consider its function. What does it do in your life?

★ Finally, think about how it makes you feel. Does it make you feel safe? Comfortable? Happy? Emotional? Taking a few minutes out of your day to be present and aware of something in your world will help you recognize the things of value, and see the magic and beauty all around you.

RULING PLANET

VENUS

Venus, the planet of love and beauty, governs Libra, which is no surprise when you consider this zodiac sign's love of luxury and looking good. Venus is associated with good taste, pleasure and attractiveness, and the Venusian influence upon Libra is aesthetically strong. After all, the pink planet is more than pleasing to the eye, and the Roman goddess of the same name was the epitome of beauty, riding to shore in her giant scallop shell. Although mainly known as the goddess of love, Venus' affiliation with attraction and material desires is just as important, and it is these aspects that come to the fore in the Libran personality.

Venus was known for her many affairs, and was easily tempted by an array of mortal and heavenly lovers. Her need for attention was great, and she cared deeply about others' perception of her. In one myth, Venus takes offence at her son Cupid's admiration of a group of earthly maidens. In retaliation, she inflicts a terrible beating upon the girls, who, black and blue, are eventually transformed into blooming violets. Librans are also concerned with how things look, and it is this need that propels them to maintain balance and harmony and seek beauty in all things.

PLANET RITUAL

RITUAL FOR INNER BEAUTY

Harness the energy of Venus by recognizing your own inner beauty with this simple but effective ritual. This is best carried out on a Friday, the day associated with this planet, and at any time when the Sun is in Libra.

You will need a full-length or small mirror.

★ Stand in front of a full-length mirror. If you haven't got one, a smaller mirror where your face is clearly visible will do.

★ Look directly into your eyes and notice how they sparkle.

★ Smile, even if you don't feel joyful. Purposely create a wide smile and see how it lights and lifts your face.

★ Stand tall with your shoulders back and lengthen your spine. Tuck your tummy in, as you inhale. Exhale and say, 'I radiate beauty. I am beauty.'

★ Repeat this affirmation at least three times. Remember to say it loudly and with meaning, then smile again and be happy and thankful for everything that makes you, you!

★ Repeat this ritual as often as you like as a reminder of your inner beauty.

LIBRA CHARACTER AND ATTRIBUTES

THE ROMANTIC

Librans know how to create a harmonious atmosphere and do their best to keep the peace at all times. Imbued with charm and the ability to adapt to any situation, these often friendly and outgoing air signs seek equilibrium in all things. Avoiding conflict is their speciality, and those born under this zodiac sign will do their best to keep everyone happy, even if that means putting their own needs to one side. While they may be people pleasers, Librans are notoriously indecisive. This is because they like to weigh up all the options, and will often change their mind several times in the course of one day. That said, most people are quick to forgive them, thanks to their natural charisma and positive attitude.

Love and attention is at the heart of the Libra ethos. They adore romance, and all of the beautiful things that it brings and tend to fall head over heels in love at first sight. This sun sign more than any other likes to adorn themselves, their home and their loved ones in luxury. Only the best will do for a Libran, and they often display creative flair when it comes to the field of design, whether that's in the home, garden or their own personal style. This zodiac sign is the ultimate glamour puss, and if something pretty catches their eye, then you can bet their head will be turned!

SCORPIO

OCTOBER 23RD TO NOVEMBER 21ST

SCORPIUS THE SCORPION

Best Time to View: July

Situated near the centre of the Milky Way, Scorpius the scorpion is a vibrant constellation comprised of many twinkling stars, including the giant red star Antares, which is located at the centre of its curving body. At least fifteen times bigger than the Sun, this enormous beauty burns with a heat so intense that it will eventually explode as a supernova. Scorpius is fairly easy to see and has many points of interest for keen astronomers, including the Cat's Paw Nebula and the Butterfly Nebula, shaped like a beautiful butterfly's wings.

CONSTELLATION MYTH

THE HUNTER AND THE SCORPION

The Greek myth that surrounds the Scorpius constellation is a reminder of the value of life on Earth, and the importance of every creature. In the story, the goddess of wild animals Artemis sought a hunting partner who could match her skill and speed. Orion the hunter was happy to oblige, and raced down from the heavens to accompany Artemis on her daily expeditions. But while Artemis only hunted to keep the balance of life and nature, Orion developed a hunger for the kill. The hunt became a game to him, and it seemed he would not stop until all of the creatures of Earth were gone.

Gaia, the goddess of all and Mother Earth, decided to intervene. After all, what would the planet be without all of its wonderful animals? Gaia sent a scorpion – an eight-legged creature with claws and a stinger that had never been seen before – to end Orion. A battle ensued, but it was short lived, for although Orion tried to pierce the creature's shell, he was not prepared for the sting of its venom. Artemis, though saddened by the loss of her companion, was relieved that the Earth's creatures were safe. The scorpion, however, was badly wounded from the encounter, and so in honour of the beast's service and bravery, Zeus turned his dying form into a beautiful star cluster, the constellation Scorpius. The shape hangs brightly for all to see, and to remind us that each and every creature has value and worth.

CREATURE OF THE BURNING STING

To the Babylonians, Scorpius was GIR.TAB, otherwise known as 'the creature with a burning sting'. This constellation was closely associated with Shamash, the god of the Sun and justice, who also held dominion in the Underworld, where the 'scorpion men', known as 'Girtablilu' could be found. These shapeshifting characters could flit between human and scorpion forms. Powerful and dark, they encapsulate the transformative nature of this zodiac sign.

In Chinese mythology, Scorpius represents the Azure Dragon of the East, which sits in the heavenly home of the Blue Emperor. The constellation's brightest star Antares was called 'Huo', meaning 'fire star', to complement its blazing red hue.

Like the Chinese dragon, the ancient Egyptians also saw this star pattern as a serpent-like being, and linked the constellation to their goddess of the Underworld, Serket, also known as Selket. A powerful deity, she was often depicted wearing a serpent-like crown and carrying an ankh.

RITUAL FOR PASSION AND GOAL SETTING

This simple writing exercise will help you tune in to your passions, and channel Scorpio's energy to create a plan to work towards your goals. You can do this at any time during Scorpio season, when the Sun is in this sign.

You will need a journal and a pen.

★ Sit with your journal and spend a couple of minutes breathing deeply to clear your mind.

★ Think about the things that are important to you. What do you want the most? What drives you forwards? Consider these questions, and write down whatever comes to mind.

★ Look at your answers and reflect upon them. Is there any common ground? Perhaps you value praise and recognition, and are motivated to aim for a promotion.

★ Think about any small steps you could take to help you turn your passion into a reality, such as learning a new skill, speaking with a mentor or meditating to focus your mind.

★ Make a list and a plan to help you move forwards.

★ Regularly take time out to reflect upon your goals, and mark any successes that you have.

RULING PLANET

PLUTO

The planet of destruction and transformation, Pluto is the perfect bedfellow for the many-layered Scorpio, being associated with rebirth and regeneration. Its influence fuels the ambition of this zodiac sign, helping these complex and deeply passionate souls move mountains and create opportunities for success. To the Romans, Pluto was the god of the Underworld, but while other mythologies tended to demonize those who took on this role, the people of Rome believed him to have two sides to his personality. Pluto was the caretaker of souls and a trusted gatekeeper, and those that entered his realm were treated fairly, depending on their deeds and misdemeanours. As time went on, Pluto grew in popularity and became associated with wealth. Every time he journeyed to the surface of the Earth, he brought with him nuggets of gold and crystals that had been mined from the rock, and so the people loved him.

He was most famous for his treatment of Orpheus, the lovelorn lyre player who came to the Underworld in search of his beau Eurydice. Orpheus played the most beautiful tune to the god, almost sending him into a deep slumber in the hope he could win back Eurydice's soul. Pluto said that Eurydice could follow Orpheus back to Earth under one condition – he must not look back at her face until they reached the other side. Orpheus agreed, but couldn't help but turn around and look back. As soon as he broke his promise, he was horrified to see his love, pale and wraithlike, slipping away from him back to the Underworld. Just like the zodiac sign under this planet's influence, Pluto was not one to cross!

PLANET RITUAL

RITUAL TO EMBRACE CHANGE

Harness the transformative nature of the planet Pluto and embrace change with this easy ritual. Perform this on any Tuesday – the day most associated with this planet – while the Sun is in Scorpio.

You will need a patch of earth or a planter filled with soil, a pair of old gloves and a trowel.

★ Pluto was known for carving out his Underworld kingdom from the soil and rocks. When digging deep he discovered gold nuggets and crystals, which he shared with his people. Connect with this energy by finding either a patch of earth in your garden or using a planter filled with soil.

★ Wearing gloves to avoid nicks or cuts, rake the surface with a trowel and then your fingers.

★ Once the soil is loosened, use your hands to scoop out a layer and dig deep into the earth. As you do this, imagine that you are burying all the things that hold you back. Imagine pouring any limitations, fears or bad habits into this space you have created in the soil.

★ Cover the hole back up with the loose soil, and say, 'I am free from restriction, and ready to embrace change.'

THE MYSTIC

Mystical Scorpios are often misunderstood, and this is partly down to their secretive, guarded nature. It's not that they're deliberately trying to confuse, they're just private souls who prefer to keep their business out of the spotlight. That said, once a Scorpio takes a liking to you, they'll be there for the long term, and are deeply loyal and passionate in relationships. These charismatic characters have an intensity about them that is magnetic. They know what they want and how to get it, and they're not afraid to play the long game. In fact, they relish the challenge and enjoy thinking one step ahead. Power is at the heart of every Scorpio, and as an emotional water sign, their fluid nature gives them hidden depths. It's likely they'll be highly intuitive, often making important decisions based on gut instincts.

Resilient and fiercely protective, once you win their trust you will have it for life, but should you cross the line or betray them, then you'll feel the sting of their tail. Like their namesake, the scorpion, they can turn when you least expect it, but this unpredictability also adds to their unique allure.

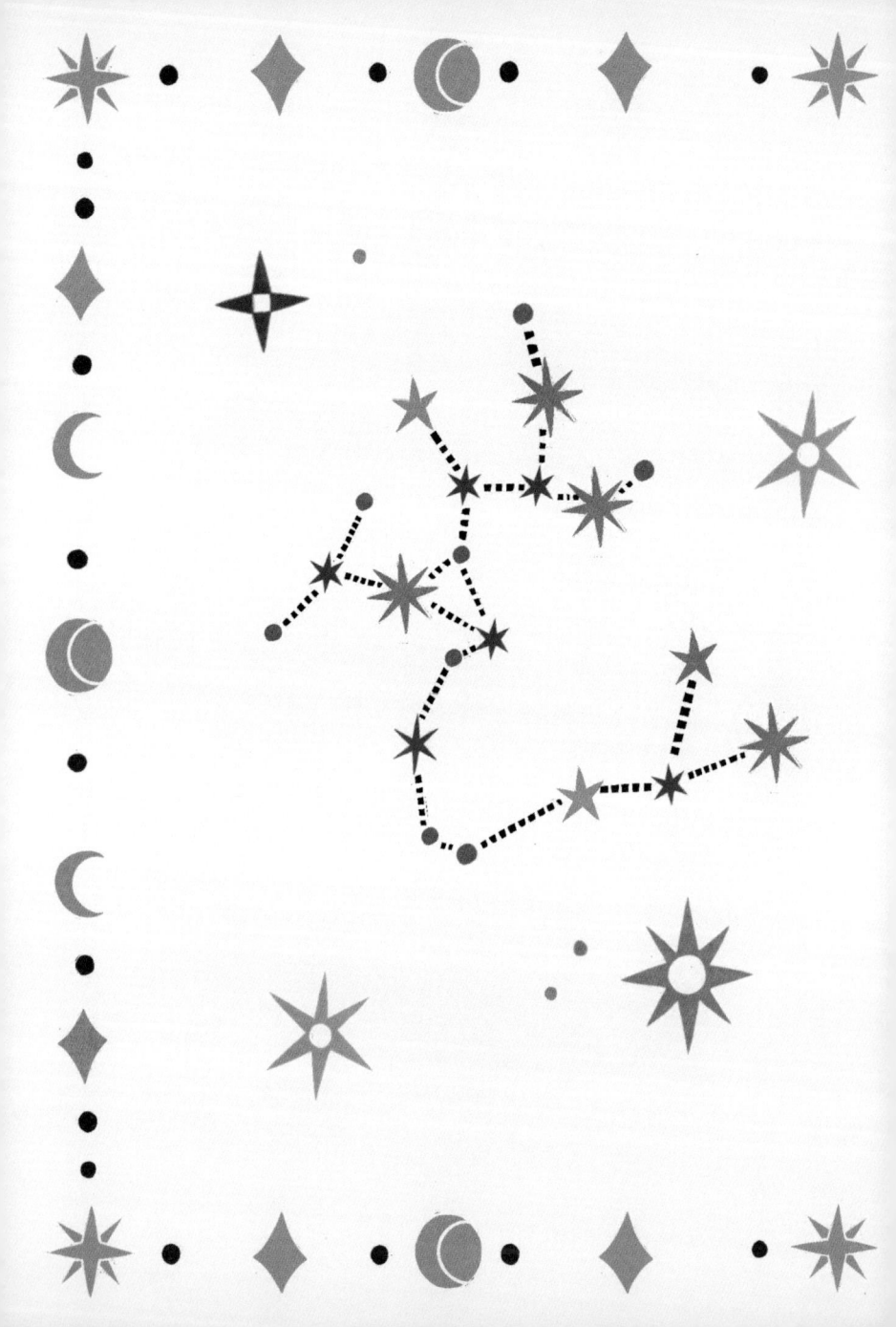

SAGITTARIUS

NOVEMBER 22ND TO DECEMBER 21ST

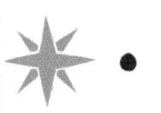

SAGITTARIUS THE ARCHER

Best Time to View: August

At the densest point of the Milky Way galaxy you will find the constellation of Sagittarius the archer lurking. With his star-clad arrow raised, he is taking aim at Antares, the bright red heart of the constellation Scorpius, in a bid to avenge the death of Orion. While mythological depictions of this constellation debate whether Sagittarius is a satyr or a centaur, today's astronomers surmise that the shape at the heart of this pattern is actually more like a glimmering teapot, with its spout tipped in the direction of the arrow. At the southern end of the bow you will find its brightest star, a swollen, shimmering beauty known as Kaus Australis.

THE CENTAUR

While most tend to think of Sagittarius as a centaur, the origins of this constellation point to a different kind of creature: a satyr called Crotus, who was responsible for the creation of the bow and arrow. According to Greek legend, Crotus was the son of Pan, god of the wild, who had an insatiable appetite for the pleasures in life. Like his father, Crotus had the hindquarters, legs and horns of a goat, but he was an altogether more thoughtful being, driven instead by a thirst for knowledge and a love of the arts.

Crotus grew up on Mount Helicon with the young muses who were nursed by his mother Eupheme. Spending time with them gave him such a deep appreciation of music, poetry and art that he soon became a skilled musician and

storyteller. Being a gentle spirit, he created the bow and arrow as a more humane way to hunt. He is also thought to have introduced the idea of giving applause to show appreciation for artistic endeavours. Despite being the son of a god, Crotus was mortal, and when he died the muses were so devastated that they begged the god Zeus to honour him, which he did, lifting Crotus' body into the skies and creating the constellation Sagittarius. Zeus added in the bow and arrow to commemorate his inventive mind, and gave him the body of horse as a nod to his freedom-loving nature.

FOLKLORE FROM AROUND THE WORLD

BRINGER OF DEATH

In Babylonian myth, Sagittarius the archer is an altogether different beast, associated with Nergal, the god of death, war and destruction, and king of the Underworld. He is still part centaur, but has two heads, one of a human and one of a panther. He also has the wings and stinger of a scorpion, etched above the horse's tail, suggesting an overlap between Sagittarius and Scorpius in the sky. The name NUN-KI was given to this star arrangement, and it is thought to represent the sacred city of Eridu on the Euphrates.

In Chinese astronomy, Sagittarius the archer contains two ancient constellations; the main one is known as Ji. Ji is the 'winnowing basket', a tool that is used to separate rice grains from chaff by shaking it gently in the air. This part of the formation is made up of four stars, Gamma, Delta, Epsilon, and Eta Sagittarii.

RITUAL TO BROADEN YOUR MIND

Sagittarians are deep thinkers who like to explore. Broaden your mind and tap into the magic of learning with this fun ritual that works with Sagittarius' spontaneous energy. You can do this as often as you like during Sagittarius season.

You will need a laptop or smartphone.

★ Open up a search engine on your laptop or smartphone.

★ Close your eyes for a second, breathe deeply, and let a word pop into your head. This could be any word, be it a place, a person, a creature or a feeling. Let the word present itself to you. If you're struggling to think of anything, pick up a book or magazine, let the pages fall open and then pick a word that stands out to you.

★ When you are ready, type the word into the search engine and see what comes up. Look at the listings and pick at least one or two to peruse. This is a fun, spontaneous exercise which works with your creative brain, while broadening your horizons and giving you the opportunity to engage with new information.

RULING PLANET

JUPITER

Larger than life and twice as powerful, the planet Jupiter is associated with power, wealth and abundance. According to the Romans, Jupiter was the king of the gods, being the biggest planet in the Solar System. The far-reaching energy of this planet and its divine counterpart is the fire beneath the feet of the restless Sagittarian, and the reason these hunters are so eager to expand their knowledge, and travel the world.

Jupiter was the god of the heavens and the leader of the Roman pantheon. His appetite for power and his many amorous triumphs are a testimony to the vibrant, go-getting energy that influences this sign of the zodiac. Known as the supreme god of Rome, he was associated with oaths and pledges, and commonly petitioned for success. While he was a benevolent god, he was also consumed with power and usurped his father Saturn from the throne. Always on the lookout for new conquests, Jupiter had an adventurous side, and it is this that propels Sagittarian explorers onwards in their quest for insight and excitement.

PLANET RITUAL

RITUAL FOR ABUNDANCE

Harness the abundance of Jupiter with this self-care ritual, which works with the power of gratitude to help you recognize blessings and expand personal wealth. This is best carried out on a Thursday, the day most associated with this planet, during Sagittarius season.

You will need a journal and a pen.

★ Find somewhere to sit and reflect with a journal and pen.

★ Think about your week so far up to this point. Consider all the things that have gone well for you, and all of the people that have made you smile. Think of all the things that you're grateful for, no matter how simple, then make a list of everything you are thankful for this week.

★ Read through the list and recall each thing in turn.

★ Notice how this lifts your mood and enriches your life. Acknowledging blessings in this way creates positive energy, which attracts more of the same.

THE EXPLORER

Expansion is the name of the game for spontaneous Sagittarians. Whether it's their field of vision, knowledge base or just a general lust for life, this centaur takes aim and will always meet the target. Constantly moving, as you might expect from the mighty and mutable bowman, Sagittarians are explorers at heart, and rarely stay in one place for long. It's knowledge that fuels the embers of this fire sign, and they like to dig deep, learning about life, philosophy and different cultures during their travels.

The freedom loving Sagittarius is virtually impossible to pin down, and if you try, they'll be off at top speed before you can whisper the word 'commitment'. It's not that they don't want a serious relationship. In truth, this sign enjoys the flirtatious, adventurous aspects of new love, and will want to know everything there is to know about their beau. Once the object of their affection has been conquered, they'll move on to the next challenge. Sagittarians have a habit of being blunt in their communications with others, and while they don't mean to offend, their straight talking, sometimes offhand approach can isolate them. That said, most people warm to the gregarious nature of this sign, and swiftly realize that it's a small price to pay for their entertaining company.

WINTER

The wheel turns towards winter as temperatures plummet, and the landscape holds its breath. There's a darkening to the vista as the earth is laid bare. The starkness, a seasonal gift, provides space to breathe and start again. We wrap up snug, donning layers so that we can explore this blank canvas. Our feet sink into deep snow, or slip over frosted ground as we traverse this new world. The skeletal trees creak in the whip of winter's winds, reaching upwards as though in search of inspiration from the skies.

Clear winter's evenings are the ideal time to see fainter stars, while bolder constellations seem brighter than ever. Taurus the bull is easy to spot, even in city skies. This vivid beast charges through the heavens, its starry V-shaped horns aimed towards Orion the hunter. Nearby you'll find mischief at hand in the twinkling guise of the Gemini twins, their heads marked by the two bright stars, Castor and Pollux.

In the zodiac calendar there are also changes afoot. Capricorn the goat arrives with the chill of the season, followed by the water carrier Aquarius. To finish this astrological triad is Pisces the fish, swimming into view for those born in the month of February.

CAPRICORN

DECEMBER 22ND TO JANUARY 19TH

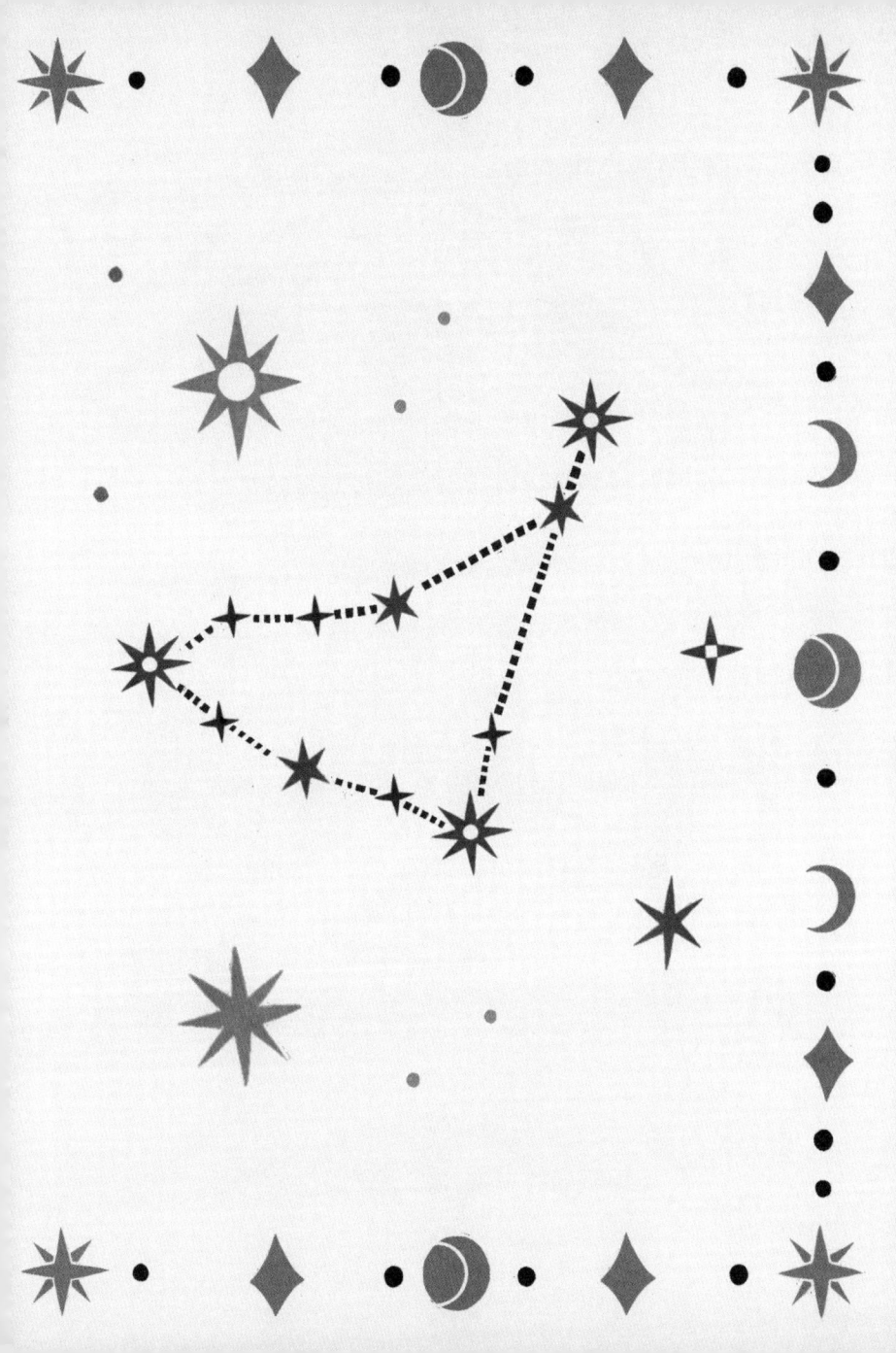

CAPRICORNUS THE GOAT

Best Time to View: September

Capricornus, meaning 'horned goat', is the smallest constellation in the zodiac, and gallops through the sky in the shape of an arrowhead, primed and pointed. It is formed of a triangular grouping of stars, the brightest of which, at the western tip, is called Giedi, derived from the Arabic for 'kid'. On closer inspection, it is actually two stars, separated by a thousand light years, despite how close they appear. Capricornus is also home to a globular cluster known as Messier 30 or the Jellyfish Cluster, which lies roughly twenty-seven thousand light years away.

THE SEA GOAT

There are varying myths associated with Capricornus, but all have one thing in common: the mythical sea goat, a creature with the upper half of a goat and the tail of a fish. Able to live on the earth as well as in the watery depths of the ocean, this creature had the ability to adapt to each environment, which is no surprise when you consider that Capricorn individuals display a similar kind of resilience in life.

In one Greek myth, the gods of Mount Olympus fled their home when the monstrous beast Typhon attacked. In a bid to escape his wrath, they shifted shape, taking on the form of different creatures to disguise their true identities. A number of the gods fled to Egypt, where Pan, the satyr-formed god of the wild, flung himself head first into the Nile. As the waters covered his body, he transformed into a half-goat, half-fish, and was able to swim to safety. It's believed that in honour of his service to Zeus in fighting the Titans, he was then transformed into the delicate constellation Capricornus.

Other Greek myths suggest that Capricornus is related to Amalthaea, the goat who suckled the infant Zeus and kept him safe in a cave on the island of Crete. The starry pattern was therefore a gift to honour her, and to commemorate the diligent care she exhibited.

GOD OF THE SEA

The ancient Sumerians had vivid imaginations and a fondness for sea creatures. They worshipped Enki, the aquatic god of wisdom and water. This sea god, who was half-goat, half-fish, lived in the Tree of Life and so was linked to both earth and water, and was represented by the goat constellation in the sky. Also the god of intelligence, creativity and art, Enki was petitioned for his ability to solve problems.

Some scholars believe that Oannes, the Babylonian god of wisdom and writing, is at the root of Capricornus, and the true representation of the goat fish. Unlike the current depiction of the sea goat, Oannes had the upper half of a man, and a fish tail.

RITUAL FOR POSITIVE PRODUCTIVITY

The sign of the goat is all about structure, and this practical ritual works with that theme to help you clear the clutter from your life. You can perform this exercise at any point during Capricorn season, and it will help you feel positive and productive.

★ Select a space within your home to organize. This could be a work area, like a desk, your wardrobe or just a corner of a room.

★ Before you begin, take a step back and look at the area. What does it say to you right now? Is it tidy, or full of clutter? How do you feel when you look at it? Set yourself a target and decide what you want to achieve before you begin. For example, set aside an hour to clear as much clutter as possible from the space.

★ Consider every item in the space and ask yourself if you really need it. Do you use it, or is it just gathering dust? Be ruthless, but also balanced. For example, if something isn't useful, but has sentimental value, then you might want to keep it, but tidy it away.

★ Once you have completed the task in the allotted time, take a look at the space and give yourself a pat on the back for achieving your goal.

RULING PLANET

SATURN

Saturn is the planet associated with rules, structure and organization, and it governs Capricorn with a firm hand. Its sobering influence gives this zodiac sign focus, and helps these formidable characters build solid foundations for the future. The Roman god Saturn was powerful and all-consuming in many ways. Associated with time, abundance and the gift of agriculture, he was revered by the Roman people, and linked to the Golden Age of peace. His success was achieved after a very prominent fall from grace.

In the early days, Saturn was a Titan and married to the goddess Rhea. Always looking to the future, he was convinced that one of his unborn children would overthrow him, and so when each one was born, he devoured them whole. Rhea, understandably mortified by this behaviour, hid the child Zeus away, unbeknown to Saturn. When Zeus was fully grown, he returned and poisoned his father, causing him to regurgitate all of the other children. At this point Saturn was cast out of the heavens in shame. Ever determined, the god knew he needed to make amends and rebuild his reputation, which he did with careful planning, eventually managing to secure his place amid the pantheon. It is this patient energy that gives Capricorns their ability to plan, and work towards goals.

PLANET RITUAL

RITUAL FOR A POSITIVE OUTLOOK

The gas-ringed planet of Saturn brings structure and foresight, and the god of the same name is linked to time. To promote insight and vision, try this simple ritual which will also help you create a positive outlook for the future. Practise this on any Saturday during Capricorn season.

★ Find somewhere comfortable to sit and reflect.

★ Close your eyes, and let your awareness fall backwards, as if you're looking at the back of your eyes.

★ Imagine there's a cinema screen in this space which suddenly bursts to life. On it, you see a vision of the future that you hope to create. Let your imagination take over at this point, and relax. Let thoughts and images present themselves on the screen.

★ If it helps, think of it as narrative, and a brief glimpse into what the future will be like. Consider each aspect of your life, from home and family, to work and love, and watch the film unfold naturally.

★ Create the future you would like in your mind and enjoy how this makes you feel.

★ When you've finished, open your eyes, give your body a shake and make a note of anything that stands out from the visualization.

★ Use the positive energy this has generated as a springboard to help you make decisions and plans for the future.

CAPRICORN CHARACTER AND ATTRIBUTES

THE RESILIENT

Regimented and resilient, Capricorn is synonymous with order and organization, which may sound boring to some, but in truth, it's the reason why these steadfast goats are so successful. Their ability to focus even when the going gets tough gives them an indestructible aura and edge against their competitors. Capricorns are all about the big picture, and often plan far into the future. These calm characters crave structure, which is partly down to their being an earth sign, as well as the influence of their governing planet Saturn.

Rules and regulations may excite the Capricorn brain, but within these constraints you'll find a mischievous character lurking. It may be hard to believe, but the sober sea goat certainly knows how to kick back, and while they won't show their wild side to everyone, their nearest and dearest are likely to have witnessed the goat in full feral party mode. These deep thinkers take their time getting to know anyone, but once they realize they can trust you, they go all in. In love, Capricorns tend to be guarded at first, as you might expect from these measured characters. Commitment is a serious matter, but once they've they tied the knot figuratively speaking, they will make every effort with their partner, and put in the work to ensure their relationship goes the distance.

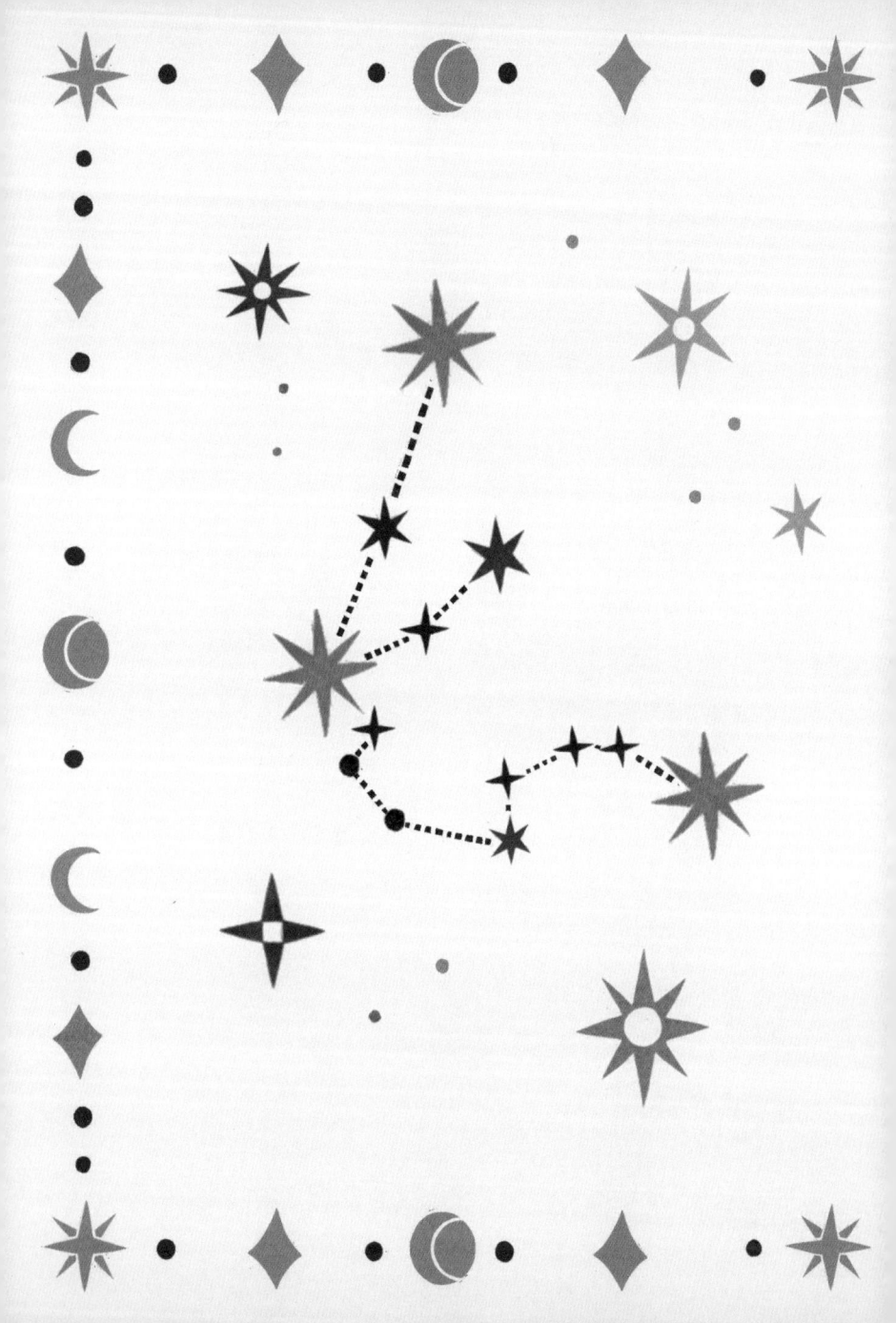

AQUARIUS

JANUARY 20TH TO FEBRUARY 18TH

CONSTELLATION DESCRIPTION

AQUARIUS THE WATER BEARER

Best Time to View: October

Though fairly large, the constellation of Aquarius the water bearer is a pallid imprint upon the night sky, and extremely hard to see. Originally mapped around two thousand years ago by the astrologer Ptolemy, this constellation, sometimes known as the cup bearer, has two significantly bright stars which are symbols of hope and luck. These sparkling beauties have the Arabic names Sadalmelik and Sadalsuud, meaning 'lucky one of the king' and 'luckiest of the lucky'. Aquarius is also home to the Delta Aquariid meteor shower, which happens every summer, but much like the constellation that houses it, is often too faint to see.

CONSTELLATION MYTH

CUP BEARER TO THE GODS

While there are many cup bearing myths, the most famous one associated with this zodiac sign and constellation is the Greek story of Ganymede, the young and handsome prince of Troy, kidnapped by the god Zeus who had assumed the form of a giant eagle. Zeus was so enamoured with his prize that he promised Ganymede eternal life, and that if he served at Mount Olympus by being cup bearer to gods, he would always be held in high regard. The boy, reassured by the god's devotion, stayed, and served water, ambrosia and wine for many years. But as was the fickle nature of Zeus, he eventually grew tired of his companion.

In some tales it was Ganymede who became frustrated at this life of servitude and downed his tools, pouring all of the

wine and water down to the Earth, angering the gods. In others, Zeus found favour in the arms of a nymph and no longer needed the prince in his bed. Whichever narrative you choose, the outcome was the same. Ganymede's services were no longer required, but he reminded Zeus of his original promise. The god stood by his word, and honoured Ganymede's loyalty by immortalizing him as a beautiful array of stars: the constellation Aquarius the water bearer.

FOLKLORE FROM AROUND THE WORLD

THE OVERFLOWING URN

To the Babylonians, the constellation of Aquarius represented an overflowing urn pouring water upon the Earth to nurture the plants and animals. They came to associate this constellation with their rainy season. Their star catalogues identify the star pattern as GU.LA, meaning 'great one'. This is thought to be a reference to Ea, god of wisdom and civilization, known to the Sumerians as Enki, the god of water.

The ancient Egyptians associated the cup bearer with Hapi, their god of the Nile. They believed that the stars outlined the deity dipping his jar into the water, and that this explained the annual flood, when the water of the Nile broke its banks.

In the Middle East the constellation was thought to be a giant bucket, sometimes depicted with a mule in place of the human outline. The ancient Arabic names for the stars in this constellation, Sadalmelik and Sadalsuud, represent different types of luck; it's thought the reason for this was that the Sun entered Aquarius at the time of the New Year, which was considered a good omen, signalling spring was on its way.

AQUARIUS RITUAL

RITUAL TO NURTURE KINDNESS

The constellation Aquarius focuses on the water bearers who give service to the gods, and are governed by their need to help, and make the world a better place. Tap into this pro-active nurturing energy with a ritual that centres on kindness. You can do this at any time during Aquarius season.

You will need a pen and paper.

★ Take piece of paper and a pen and sit for a moment. Think about what kindness means to you, and how you might embody this in your actions with others.

★ Consider all the little things you can do to make someone's life better, whether that's at home, at work, with friends or in your community. Consider simple things such as helping someone with a chore, offering encouragement or being there to listen and support a friend or colleague.

★ Make a list of these ideas.

★ Place the list somewhere prominent where you can see it every day, and make a point of integrating some of these ideas into your daily activities.

RULING PLANET

URANUS

Often thought of as the planet of disruption, Uranus is unpredictable, unconventional and rebellious, much like the sign it governs. The planet is associated with ingenuity and adventure, and has an innovative influence on Aquarius, promoting change and new perspectives.

To the Romans, Uranus was known as father of the sky and air. He was the original consort of the goddess Gaia, Mother Earth. After Gaia created the world, she created Uranus to be her companion. Depicted as a magnificent man with flowing blue-green robes, he was sometimes called the rainmaker, and the water that flowed from him nurtured the earth. Uranus was powerful and intellectual, but could be mistrustful, and when his children were born, he began to obsess that they might overthrow him. Fearing for his throne, he kidnapped most of his children, imprisoning them in Tartarus, the pit of hell. In revenge, Gaia crafted a sickle from a lump of stone, which her son Cronus used to cut off his father's genitals. The blood that flowed from the wound created the giants, the Meliae and the Furies, while the genitals, which were tossed into the ocean, gave birth to the goddess Venus. Even in death, Uranus had found a way to make change, just like the pioneering nature of Aquarius.

PLANET RITUAL

RITUAL FOR A FRESH PERSPECTIVE

This creative ritual uses the inventive power of words to reveal a fresh perspective, and open your mind to new ways of thinking. It taps into the innovative, change-bringing aspects of the planet Uranus and can be carried out at any time during Aquarius season.

You will need your favourite book and a pen and paper.

★ Take one of your favourite books, and either flip it open and read the first line at the top of the page, or turn to the end of the book and read the last line.

★ On your piece of paper, write this line of text at the top of a page as if it's the first line, and then let your imagination take over and continue the narrative. You don't have to write a lot, just a few sentences or a paragraph is enough to open your mind, and trigger creativity.

★ You can also use this exercise if you have something that you need to present or write, and you want to adopt a fresh approach. Simply pick a line from what you have already prepared, and come at it from a different angle, letting your imagination flow and see what transpires.

AQUARIUS CHARACTER AND ATTRIBUTES

THE INNOVATOR

Groundbreaking Aquarius is a sign that wants to make waves. While they're often thought of as water babies, Aquarians are governed by the element of air, making them highly intellectual and big thinkers. These innovative characters don't do anything by halves, and are likely to be inspired by humanitarian causes where they can really make a difference. They'll go all out for something they believe in, and will have an abundance of ideas to implement.

Quirky and individual, these colourful characters are easy to spot, as they stand out from the crowd. Their style is unique, as is the way they move through the world. Aquarians can often appear lofty and aloof, but this comes from a head in the clouds attitude, rather than any real malice. They're so consumed with world issues and how they can make a difference, that they often forget to pay attention to those close to them. In love, Aquarians are creative, and can be thoughtful when they're not totally immersed in personal projects or ventures. These water bearers like to serve the greater good, but they can also be hard-headed at times, thanks to the fixed nature of their sign. This means that once they've made their mind up about something, it's very hard to persuade them otherwise. Rebellious and inventive, life is almost always unpredictable and exciting in their company.

PISCES

FEBRUARY 19TH TO MARCH 20TH

PISCES THE FISH

Best Time to View: November

One of the first constellations to be catalogued, Pisces the fish, depicted as two fish tied together by a cord around their tails, is a whisper against the backdrop of the night sky. Incredibly hard to see despite being one of the largest constellations, it has many objects of interest to astronomers, including the spiral galaxy Messier 74. This cosmic spinning wheel of gas is a smaller version of the Milky Way that produces new stars within its twirling arms. The brightest star in the Pisces constellation is Eta Piscium.

CONSTELLATION MYTH

THE GOLDEN FISH

The myth attributed to the constellation Pisces is a heroic story that demonstrates that it doesn't matter what size or shape you are; you can still make a difference. According to the Greek legend, the monster Typhon had escaped his earthly prison, and went on a rampage through Mount Olympus. Most of the gods fled, some even changing shape to hide from his wrath, but Aphrodite, goddess of love and beauty, and her son Eros were nowhere to be found. Zeus did not know how to reach them, so he put a call out to all of the creatures of the Earth and asked for their help.

Meanwhile, Aphrodite and her son were languishing by a woodland pool, unaware of the chaos above. Typhon soon caught their scent and charged through the woods towards them, but two fish happened to be swimming in the pool, and offered to carry the heavenly beings to safety. Clambering upon their backs, Aphrodite used a rope to tie their tails together so that they would not lose each other. The fish were strong and swift, and followed the stream towards the river and then to the sea, carrying their charges to safety. In some versions of the myth, Aphrodite and Eros transform into the golden fish themselves. In honour of Aphrodite and Eros' watery escape, the fish were transformed into a glimmering pattern of stars, and lifted into the sky where they would swim for eternity.

FOLKLORE FROM AROUND THE WORLD

THE FISH OF THE NILE

Known as 'the Tails' to the ancient Babylonian astronomers, the connecting cord that binds the fish together in the heavens was considered the most important part of this constellation. The star at the point of the cord was known as Alrescha, 'the bright star of the ribbon of the fishes', and it was thought to be the lead star. The cord itself represented the celestial bond, and marked the spring equinox.

The ancient Egyptians called the Pisces constellation the 'Fish of the Nile,' and the image of entwined fish were often found carved into coffin lids.

RITUAL FOR DREAMWORK

This ritual taps into the subconscious mind and helps you tune in to the prophetic energy of Pisces. Start practising this ritual near the beginning of the Pisces season.

You will need a piece of aquamarine, a notepad and a pen.

★ Invest in a piece of aquamarine. This stone is associated with water and the sign of Pisces. Its calming fluid energy will lull you into sleep and stimulate your subconscious.

★ Hold the stone in both hands before bed. Take a long, slow breath in through the nose, and as you exhale through the mouth, set your intention to have an insightful dream. Let the breath seep from your lips into the stone.

★ Repeat this for another couple of breaths, and then place the stone beneath your pillow.

★ Keep a notepad and pen by your bed so that if you wake in the night you can record any fragments of dream. Note down what you can remember and continue this practice throughout Pisces season.

★ At the end of Pisces season, read and reflect upon your dream musings. You may notice a pattern or theme that takes prominence, or tallies with events in your life.

RULING PLANET

NEPTUNE

The planet Neptune is associated with intuition and illusion. It governs the surreal, and is linked to the imagination. This ice giant of the skies was thought to be the god of the sea and fresh water, and he lived in a golden palace upon the ocean floor, according to the Romans. While he wasn't as popular with the people as some of other more predominant land and sky deities, he still had an important function. Many believed that it was Neptune who shaped the Earth, letting the waters of his emotions overflow to carve a path through the barren land.

The underwater realm that he inhabited was a place of magic and monsters where nothing was quite as it seemed, and this mystical energy flows into the psyche of the Pisces mind. Those born under this sun sign often find themselves carried away by their emotions, and have a tendency to let their imagination run away with them, just like the god of the same name, who in general was an affable character, but at times could let his feelings overflow. While Pisceans are generally amenable and caring, a turbulent stew of emotions brews beneath the surface. This is reminiscent of Neptune's domain of the sea, which often appears calm upon the surface, but can change at the turn of the breeze into a tempestuous tyrant, and a dangerous place to be. That said, the ocean is a place of mystery and secrets, and this too is evident in Piscean characters, who bring an air of enchantment to everything they do.

PLANET RITUAL

RITUAL FOR ENERGY AND POSITIVITY

The fluid watery energy of Neptune can help you release pent-up emotion and get rid of negativity. This simple ritual is a great way to start the day with a clean slate, so that you feel calm and energized. You can practise this any time during Pisces season, but it's particularly effective when the Moon is waning (getting smaller).

★ Stand in the shower and before you turn it on, bring to mind all of the things that might be weighing you down, such as any thoughts, feelings and frustrations that are bothering you.

★ Turn on the shower and close your eyes.

★ Concentrate on what you can feel as the water hits the top of your head and cascades downwards over your body. Feel it washing over your skin and imagine that as it flows, it is cleansing you of any negative energy, drawing it from your body and mind.

★ Breathe deeply and continue to enjoy the sensation of freedom as your body, mind and soul are cleansed and refreshed.

THE DREAMER

Gentle and loving, the personable Pisces is the last sign of the zodiac, and as such, has absorbed all of the lessons learnt by the other eleven signs, making it the most open and empathic. These sensitive lovelies can be bruised by life's knocks because they take things to heart They care so much that their emotions often lead them to a dark place as they take on the woes of the world. Being a water sign, they're supremely emotional, and highly intuitive. These ethereal fish have highly tuned psychic senses and are most likely to have prophetic dreams. In fact, the dream world, be it the illusory realm of daydreams or deep slumber, plays an important role in their day-to-day life. Pisceans pay more attention to dreams than any other sign, and will often make key decisions based upon signs and symbols they perceive from the universe.

Love is also of paramount importance to this dreamy fish, and they are on a constant search for their soul mate. When they find the one, they'll shower them with romance, and layer so much affection upon this individual that it can be overwhelming. They're not trying to cause alarm; they just like to make people feel special. With a highly active imagination and the ability to engage with the world on many levels, Pisceans are creative and naturally attuned to the arts, and need an outlet that allows them to put their otherworldly attributes to good use.

STAR BATHING

The blanket of the night sky is the perfect bedfellow if you're looking to find serenity and instil a sense of peace in your life. Immersing yourself in the starry canopy above your head has many positive benefits on body, mind and soul. At its core, it helps you reconnect with the natural world, which soothes the mind and acts like a personal charger, imbuing you with celestial energy. Being at one with the universe in this way reminds you not only of your place in the world and the value that you bring, but also of the greater potential out there. The cosmos is limitless and vast, and simply sitting in its presence and absorbing the beauty will inspire you to think big, and dream even bigger.

Star bathing is a mindful practice that you can do to help you connect with the universe and experience a greater sense of wellbeing.

WHAT TO DO

★ Find a spot beneath the stars somewhere dark and away from urban light, and lay a blanket on the ground.

★ Lay down and feel the weight of your body press into the earth. Know that the ground anchors you, holding you safe within its gravitational grip.

★ Relax, and take a few long, slow breaths. Feel the gentle rise and fall of your chest, and listen to your breath.

★ Look up at the sky and let your gaze soften as you take in the starry patterns. Don't force your stare, just enjoy letting the scene wash over you. This is not about identifying constellations or groupings, it's simply about being in the moment, and experiencing the beauty of the skyscape.

★ With every breath, draw in the vista. Imagine pulling it towards you.

★ Feel the air circulate around you, and know that this is all that separates you from the magnificence of the celestial blanket above.

★ Breathe, and connect with the magical energy of the stars. Lose yourself in the patterns, and let them come to life in your imagination. If your mind begins to drift and other worries surface, bring your attention back to the stars and let their twinkling beauty wash over you.

★ When you've finished, give yourself a moment to disconnect and come back to earth. Give your body a gentle shake, stretch your limbs, and take a couple of deep, energizing breaths.

HOW TO STARGAZE

You don't have to be an export or a professional astronomer to appreciate the delights of the sky at night. All you need is a clear view and the willingness to be still and in the moment.

You will need something to sit on, binoculars (optional), a notebook and pen (optional) and a smartphone.

★ To begin, find a good viewing spot where you will be comfortable and have a clear view of the sky. A location away from urban light and other city distractions is ideal, like at the top of a hill or in a forest clearing.

★ Wrap up warm and take something to sit or lie on. While you can see many wonders of the night sky unaided, a pair of decent binoculars will help you pick out specific planets and constellations. You could also take a notebook and pen with you to jot down what you see or just record your thoughts. Your smartphone is also helpful; try a stargazing app to help you identify stars and planets.

★ To help you navigate the night sky, try to plan what you'd like to see. Start with something simple like identifying the North Star, or the constellation Orion, which is fairly easy to see on a clear night. Once you have located these, you can move on to some of the other planets and stars.

★ Enjoy the experience. You might only notice a couple of stars at the beginning, but you'll begin to pick out others as you familiarize yourself with the night sky.

PLANET SPOTLIGHT

The planets in the Solar System orbit the Sun, and they all move at different rates, which means that visibility varies at different times of year, and they are never in the same place. There are at least five planets that you can see with the naked eye if you have the time and patience. The five brightest planets in the night sky are Venus, Mars, Jupiter, Mercury and Saturn, with Mercury being the hardest to see, as it's the closest to the Sun and affected by its glare.

You'll know when you spot a planet because while it may look like a pinprick of light in the distance, it doesn't twinkle like a star, which is much further away and affected by the Earth's atmosphere. Astronomical apps can help by alerting you when a planet might be visible, and giving an indication of its location.

MERCURY

Mercury is the first planet in the Solar System and the closest to the Sun – around a third of the distance between the Sun and Earth. Despite its proximity, Mercury doesn't retain much heat, because of its weak atmosphere and temperatures that fluctuate wildly throughout the day. Small, but still prominent at the moment, this planet is slowly shrinking in size. It's thought to be approximately nine miles smaller than it was four billion years ago. Light grey in colour, Mercury's surface is covered in craters like the Moon.

Mercury is associated with movement, change and communication, and governs the signs Gemini and Virgo.

VENUS

Venus is often called Earth's sister planet because it is so similar in size and mass. Despite this likeness, Venus is uninhabitable, with temperatures reaching a scorching 464°C (867°F), due to a high concentration of carbon dioxide in the atmosphere. It's the second closest planet to the Sun, and while its surface is shrouded in opaque clouds, it is the third brightest object in the Solar System as seen from the Earth.

Venus is the planet of love, beauty and sexuality, and rules over Taurus and Libra.

MARS

Mars is the second smallest planet in the Solar System, but what it lacks in size it makes up for in brightness. Its vibrant red colouring comes from the large amount of iron oxide present in the soil. The winds on Mars blow dust from the earth upwards, giving the sky a pink tinge. Being the fourth planet from the Sun in our Solar System, it's also extremely cold, with temperatures averaging at a chilly -65°C (-85°F).

Mars, like its namesake the god of war, is linked to instinct, assertiveness and survival, and governs the sign of Aries.

JUPITER

The fifth planet from the Sun, this gas giant is approximately eleven times larger than the Earth, making it by far the biggest planet. It has seventy-nine known moons to itself! Jupiter is also the fastest rotating planet, spinning at a speed of around 45,300 km/h (28,150 miles). This rapid rotation has caused the planet's poles to flatten, so it appears bulged at the centre. One of Jupiter's best known features, the Great Red Spot, was first identified in 1665 by the Italian astronomer Giovanni Cassini. Located south of the equator, it is around 24,000 km (15,000 miles) in diameter, which is big enough to contain the Earth and a couple of other planets.

Jupiter's qualities are those of power, wealth and abundance, and it rules over the sign of Sagittarius.

SATURN

The second largest planet in the Solar System, and the sixth from the Sun, Saturn is comprised of hydrogen and helium, with a dense core of iron and nickel. It is mostly known for its unique rings, which are thought to have been created from broken asteroids that shattered when they encountered Saturn's powerful gravity. Winds on Saturn are extremely high, reaching up to 1,800 km/h (1120 miles) at the equator.

Saturn is connected with rules, structure, productivity and organization, and governs the sign of Capricorn.

URANUS

This ice giant is the seventh planet from the Sun, with a small rocky core surrounded by water, methane and ammonia. Thought to have formed around four and a half billion years ago, it's likely it was nearer the Sun at that time, but then moved further away. Uranus is the third largest planet in the Solar System, and has thirteen planetary rings. The reason it appears to be spinning sideways is because its equator is at a right angle to its orbit. It's thought an earlier collision with a planet or object the size of Earth might have caused this.

Uranus is associated with sudden change, and is seen as the planet of rebellion and originality. It rules the sign Aquarius.

NEPTUNE

The planet Neptune is the farthest from the Sun, and is cloaked in a vivid blue cloud haze. It is the smallest of the three gas giants, but it is also the densest and the fourth largest planet in the Solar System. While it is made up of ice and gas and impossible to stand on, its levels of gravity are similar to those on Earth. Neptune has six faint rings, which are incredibly hard to see, and fourteen moons. The most famous is Triton, which it's thought was captured by the planet's gravitational pull.

Neptune is the planet of illusion, fantasy and idealism, often associated with dreamers. It governs the sign of Pisces.

PLUTO

Diminutive Pluto is known as a dwarf planet, and is much smaller than the Moon, being only 1,400 miles wide. Despite its tiny size compared to other planets in the Solar System, it has five moons, the largest being Charon, which is roughly the same size as Pluto. It has a thin atmosphere made up of nitrogen, methane and carbon monoxide, and an interesting landscape that features white-capped mountains, valleys and craters. Pluto's orbit around the Sun is elliptical and tilted, which means that on occasion it is actually closer to the Sun than the planet Neptune.

Pluto is associated with death, destruction and transformation, and is sometimes seen as a sign of foreboding. It rules over the sign of Scorpio.

MONTHLY GUIDE TO THE BEST TIME TO SEE CONSTELLATIONS

(NORTHERN HEMISPHERE)

Stars rise and fall in the sky, and move by around ninety degrees each season. As a result, the constellations you can see will vary in visibility from month to month.

While some of the constellations listed below can be seen over three or four months at a time, this guide gives you an idea of which zodiac constellations are the most prominently visible each month in the night sky, giving you the best chance of seeing them.

January	Taurus
February	Gemini
March	Cancer
April	Leo
May	Virgo
June	Libra
July	Scorpius
August	Sagittarius
September	Capricornus
October	Aquarius
November	Pisces
December	Aries

ABOUT THE AUTHOR

A professional storyteller with a keen interest in mythology, spirituality and the natural world, Alison Davies is the author of over sixty books, including *The Mystical Year*, *The Lunar Year* and *The Self-Care Year*. She also runs writing workshops at universities across the United Kingdom.

ACKNOWLEDGEMENTS

I would like to thank the wonderful team at Quadrille for helping to create such a special book. In particular, I'd like thank my editors Harriet Butt and Ellie Spence for their talent and skill, the designer Alicia House for helping to shape my words and make them stand out on the page, and also the wonderful illustrator, Megan Ivy Griffiths, for the magical illustrations.